As a middle school writing workshop teacher who has just begun experimenting with the flipped classroom model, this book is a godsend! Dana and Sonja prove that flipped lessons support the writing workshop tenets, and show us how these lessons fit into the routines of our buzzing, magical workshops. They provide you with all of the resources you need to apply this new teaching method, and forever change the way you teach writing.

—DEVAN FITZPATRICK, lower school teacher, Fay School, Southborough, MA

With *Flip Your Writing Workshop* you will learn how a few carefully crafted flipped minilessons can meet your students' needs **when** they need them! Dana and Sonja share a range of tools, from easy-to-use to more complex, as well as a framework that will guide you every step of the way. An added bonus is the invitation to step into Dana and Sonja's writing workshops to see how they created, implemented, evaluated, and improved their own flipped writing minilessons as well as the student responses that are included for each lesson.

—FRAN MCVEIGH, literacy consultant and adjunct instructor

Flip Your Writing Workshop is a step-by-step, practical guide to creating a flipped English classroom. Johansen and Cherry-Paul provide tools for teachers new to flipped learning, as well as teachers who are not "tech comfortable." Technology is often the biggest barrier for teachers starting to flip, and this book helps demystify the process. Writing workshop is a powerful pedagogical tool, and the authors incorporate technology in a clear and imaginative way to make it manageable for any teacher. This book is a great resource for teachers looking to flip their class!

—CHERYL MORRIS, teacher and flipped learning leader

As a teacher who has also struggled to make time for every single writer in my classroom, I was drawn to *Flip Your Writing Workshop* by the fact that Dana and Sonja start out with *hope* and a can-do attitude. They acknowledge both the promise and potential pitfalls of implementing flipped learning, and they offer guidance every step of the way. Flipped learning is about reimagining the most valuable resource we teachers have at our disposal: time.

—MEENOO RAMI, author of *Thrive*

In this book, Dana and Sonja offer an insider's look into their flipped writing workshops. By sharing stories from their classrooms, examples from students, videos of flipped writing lessons, step-by-step instructions, and technology tips, they expertly demonstrate how a blended learning approach can easily be put into place in today's busy classroom. If you're searching for time, differentiate your instruction, and assist mor all while promoting student agency, the *Flip Your Writing Workshop: A Blended*

—LISA EICKHOLDT, author of *Learning*

Flip Your Writing Workshop is a clear, unintimidating, practical guide for *real* teachers to understand the "hows" and "whys" of incorporating flipped learning into each stage of writers' workshop as it applies to a *real* classroom. Johansen and Cherry-Paul take the true challenges of the classroom and offer a practical, step-by-step solution that accounts for varied teaching environments and situations. This is an instructional guide on how to use flipped learning to meet the needs of all students, foster student choice, set goals, and empower independence in class and at home. As a middle school literacy specialist, it will be a resource I recommend to teachers again and again.

—ABBE HOCHERMAN, Pollard Middle School literacy specialist

If the idea of flipping lessons in your writing workshop is appealing to you, but you are not sure where to begin, the answer is in this book. I have seen firsthand how Dana and Sonja's approach to writing workshop transforms students' writing. As a technology facilitator, I appreciate resources that present innovative approaches to learning and make teachers comfortable. Dana and Sonja have done just that. I am thrilled to have this resource at my disposal when consulting with writing teachers interested in incorporating technology in a meaningful, impactful way.

—CHRISTOPHER KEOGH, technology facilitator, Hastings-on-Hudson Union-Free School District

Flip *your* writing workshop

A **Blended Learning** Approach

DANA JOHANSEN AND SONJA CHERRY-PAUL

HEINEMANN
Portsmouth, NH

Heinemann

361 Hanover Street

Portsmouth, NH 03801–3912

www.heinemann.com

Offices and agents throughout the world

Library of Congress Cataloging-in-Publication Data

Names: Johansen, Dana, author. | Cherry-Paul, Sonja, author.

Title: Flip your writing workshop : a blended learning approach / Dana Johansen and Sonja Cherry-Paul.

Description: Portsmouth, NH : Heinemann, 2016. | Includes bibliographical references.

Identifiers: LCCN 2016003871 | ISBN 9780325076744

Subjects: LCSH: Composition (Language arts)—Study and teaching (Elementary). | Composition (Language arts)—Study and teaching (Middle school). | Blended learning. | Individualized instruction.

Classification: LCC LB1576 .J5857 2016 | DDC 372.62/3—dc23

LC record available at http://lccn.loc.gov/2016003871

Acquisitions Editor: Holly Kim Price

Development Editor: Alan Huisman

Production Editor: Patty Adams

Cover Design: Suzanne Heiser

Interior Design: Shawn Girsberger

Typesetter: Shawn Girsberger

Manufacturing: Steve Bernier

Printed in the United States of America on acid-free paper

20 19 18 17 16   PPC   1   2   3   4   5

To all of our students, for your vision, innovation, and enthusiasm.

Thank you for guiding us along this journey.

Contents

CHAPTER 3 ⋮ Drafting: Writing with Intent   26

CHAPTER 4 ⋮ Revising: Seeing Our Work Again   40

CHAPTER 5 ⋮ Editing: Polishing with Flare   53

CHAPTER 6 : **Publishing: Reflecting and Celebrating   68**

ACKNOWLEDGMENTS

It is an honor to have the opportunity to write for educators. As full-time teachers ourselves, we don't take this responsibility lightly. This book is a product of our collaboration and our drive to continually hone our teaching practices. We are deeply grateful for the support and encouragement of so many who make this work possible.

We are so grateful for Lucy Calkins, our mentor and advisor at Teachers College, Columbia University. Thank you for sharing your expertise, your time, and your humor with us. The encouragement and opportunities you've provided continue to shed light on the importance of being a practitioner.

Thank you to all of our students, who continually inspire us each day. After so many years of teaching, we are still excited to enter our classrooms each morning because of your commitment and passion toward learning. This book is a commemoration of your hard work, and we are just so proud of you and your growth, particularly as writers. Thanks also to the parents, administrators, and colleagues who have supported our work.

To everyone in the Heinemann family, a thunderous round of applause! Many thanks to Holly Kim Price for your insight, patience, and commitment to this project. Thank you for being such a good listener and for helping us to see the light! We are so grateful for the exceptional talents of Alan Huisman, Sarah Fournier, Patty Adams, Suzanne Heiser, Shawn Girsberger, Brett Whitmarsh, Kim Cahill, Elizabeth Tripp, and Steve Bernier.

Finally, thank you to the incredible staff at our local Panera Bread! We've written many drafts sitting at our favorite table in your cozy restaurant. Your friendly staff, delicious egg sandwiches, and creamy hot chocolate have sustained us throughout the writing process.

From Dana

This book would not be here without the loving support of my father, Rick Johansen, who has always encouraged me to learn with technology. It all began with that first Speak & Spell, Dad! I'm thankful for the support of my family: Mom, Steve, Kathy, Bonnie, Erin, and Nick. Thank you for all your love, encouragement, and never-ending patience for my 6 a.m. writing sessions.

Thank you for all your support to the students, parents, teachers, and administrators at Greenwich Academy, especially Molly King, Becky Walker, Nina Hanlon, Mark Feiner, and Edwina Foster. Thank you to Jeanette Tyndall, who gave me *Writing Down the Bones* and *Bird by Bird*. You told me that these books would change my life as a writer, and you were right. Maureen Mooney, you are my soundboard for the good, bad, and ridiculous ideas that pop into my mind. Thank you for all of our lunchtime think-tank sessions. Connie Blunden, my Friday-night sushi date, you are passionate about teaching and changing the world. You inspire me! Thank you to my fabulous Group V teaching team: Meagan Jones, Sarah Popescu, Catherine Cronin, and Kate Lee. I am so grateful to work closely with you each and every day. Thank you to Devan FitzPatrick. You always get excited about trying new ideas for using technology in writing workshop, no matter the challenge. Thank you for our walks and iced tea chats. Thank you to Nicole DeRosa for our Boxcar dinners and butcher-block-paper sessions. You inspired me to try flipped learning in my classroom; I am ever grateful.

Heartfelt thanks go to the technology faculty at Greenwich Academy. You are the ones who inspire, encourage, and bring new ideas to our school. Katherine Schulze, thank you for continually saying yes! A Triple Letter Word Score–size thank-you goes out to Joe Knowlton and Melissa Cassis, who always help me get the tech working. Not only are you both fierce Words with Friends competitors, but you are always there when I need you. Finally, a loving thank you to Yumi Nakanishi. You encouraged me to attend conferences and present my ideas about using technology in the classroom. This book would not exist without you! You gave me the courage to use technology in my writing lessons and push through the challenges. Thank you!

From Sonja

Thank you, Frank, for everything—for your patience, love, and wisdom. You are the anchor that roots me when life spirals and you are the wind that enables me to soar. Imani, you are my heartbeat. Thank you for sharing your technical savviness with me and for keeping me "on point" in all things!

To my parents, Edward and Mary, and to Eddie, my brother, thanks for your love and support. I'm grateful for all of my family, especially Jason, Nikki, Ella, and Nina. My best writing breaks have been spent laughing and sharing Chinese food with you. Thank you, Uncle Wen, for making sure my work has a special place in your local library.

Thank you to Tom Hatch and Karen Hammerness for listening and for guiding me academically and professionally. Thanks to Tara Lencl (Wifey) for your enthusiasm, encouragement, and for appreciating Big Ma's cornbread dressing as much as I do each Thanksgiving. To Carolyn Denton, thanks for long road trips, long talks, long laughter, and for endless opportunities for "You know what I've never done?"

To Jocelyn and Jodi, thanks for restoring my sanity and for bringing soccer into my life. Thank you to Erica Finegan for being the best February-break shopping buddy. Nobody does "This old thing?" better than you! Thanks to Abbe Hocherman for continuing our "coffee talks" across two states and for always being game to talk shop and dive into what's new in teaching. And to Jenice Mateo-Toledo for keeping it real, always. It's so wonderful to be on this academic journey with you as we strive to grab the brass ring.

Huge thanks to Gail Kipper and to Farragut Middle School for your support and encouragement. Special thanks to Chris Keogh, for your brilliance and continual support with technology. Flipping lessons would not be possible without your help with navigating the obstacles. Thank you for allowing me to dream big and then helping to bring my visions to reality. If only our classrooms were closer! And to Patrick Theodule, thank you for always taking my calls and for solving both minor and major technical glitches swiftly.

INTRODUCTION

Flipped learning helps students work at their own pace, set their own learning goals, and work with you to assess progress and set goals for the future. Flipped learning helps ensure that students can access instruction when they need it in order to continue moving forward.

— Dana and Sonja

Each year we set up our classrooms and prepare to teach writing. It's a time brimming with hope and promise. Polished floors sparkle. Desks are grouped in clusters, tables positioned for optimal student collaboration. The meeting area is surrounded by picture books to be used as mentor texts. We plan our first series of minilessons, the writing rituals and routines we'll introduce. We stock our shelves with markers and chart paper, envisioning the anchor charts we'll create with our students and where they'll hang.

We close our eyes and see a writing workshop buzzing with the sound of pencils flying across notebook pages, fingers tapping on keyboards, and students conferring with us or their writing partners. We imagine minilessons, small-group work, and assessments working together to meet the needs of all learners. No one is clamoring for help. No one is staring blankly at his or her notebook. No one is saying, "I'm finished. Now what?" Everyone is working diligently and quietly, accomplishing all we've imagined. . . .

Wait! What? This may be how classrooms are portrayed in books and videos and at professional development conferences, but they look very different in real life!

Our workshops are not picture-perfect. Creating an environment in which every student's needs are met and each learner is moving forward is a daily challenge. More often than not, a few students sit and stare; they haven't generated any ideas for their writing and are still at square one. When we take a closer look at the students who *are* working diligently, we notice some of them need to rethink ideas that are not rich enough to sustain their writing throughout the unit. Others need to rein in ideas that are too broad. And two or three are several steps ahead of their classmates (and sometimes us!); they've mastered the skills we're teaching and are ready to move on to something more challenging. There are also students we know are struggling, but we're not sure what's causing the trouble or how to help. Each learner has different writing goals and is moving at her or his own pace. Our writing workshops feel more chaotic than calm.

But we love the ebb and flow. Even though we wish we could do some days over, we know learning does not happen in lockstep, with everyone working at the same pace. Teaching is a daily orchestration directed at meeting the needs of all our students. We continue to ask, "How can I create an organized, structured, rigorous, and highly managed setting in which all learners can work at their own pace and learn the skills they need to move forward?" Each day we set goals for ourselves and with our students, and we work hard to achieve them. Given the wide variety of learners' needs, as well as the time constraints we face, it can be challenging to see progress. We turned to flipped learning to address some of the challenges in our writing workshops and are delighted with the results.

Technology as a Teaching Tool

No two teachers are the same in their approach and feeling toward technology. We each equip our wheelhouse with hardware and software with which we feel confident and comfortable. Following are brief synopses of our journeys as digital learners and teachers and how this led to creating flipped lessons in our writing workshops.

Dana

Writing workshop fills my classroom with energy, creativity, and passion. Technology is a relatively new aspect, one that provides greater organization and opportunities for collaboration and assessment. I love technology, and I like thinking about ways to incorporate it into my curriculum. Learning to use new forms of technology is a rewarding challenge! If I'm having trouble with a particular platform, I ask a colleague for help, check out tutorials online, or fiddle until I figure it out. I also enjoy the added challenge of learning new ways to use technology in the classroom. It breathes new life into the room and the curriculum because it forces me to rethink my teaching.

My experience with technology goes back twenty years, to high school. I didn't have an email account, and very few people had cell phones ("for emergencies only"). My teachers didn't use technology in the classroom, other than occasionally wheeling in a TV/VCR combo on a stand. No one documented her life on a blog, an Instagram account, or a Facebook page. Computers were used for word processing and printing final drafts.

Jump ahead to 2004, my first year of teaching fourth grade. It was also my first time attending the Teachers College Reading and Writing Project's summer conference, in Chappaqua, New York. I excitedly incorporated the workshop approach into my classroom. I had an email account (though my students did not) and a cell phone (but rarely used it). Technology in my classroom consisted of five turquoise Apple desktop computers on a long table, which students used for word processing and publishing their final drafts. I would announce that it was time to switch to make sure students took turns typing their final pieces. Neatly printed copies hung proudly on our writing workshop bulletin board, and students assembled photocopied, plastic-bound anthologies of their stories.

Today, technology has changed everything about the daily routines in my middle school writing workshop. I use my cell phone to update the classroom blog, send tweets to authors, and take notes during writing conferences. Most of my students have personal email accounts and bring their cell phones to school each day. They use technology for communication, entertainment, and content creation.

Google Drive, WordPress, and Zaption allow them to exercise authentic writing practices, collaborate, and reach real audiences.

In connection with this new technology, I search for ways to maximize the workshop experience, differentiate my instruction, and create an environment in which students can find the information they need on their own.

Sonja

Traditionalist. Technophobe. Luddite. When you hear these terms, do you slide down in your chair, hoping to remain inconspicuous? Or perhaps you pull out your smartphone to show you're with it, you know what's happening (good move!). Or maybe you're a proud, card-carrying old fogy. I've enacted each of these scenarios.

When I was in elementary school, the closest I came to having a digital experience was using a calculator. In middle school, I took my Walkman everywhere and enjoyed playing with the Atari console I shared with my brother. In high school, the excitement continued as I learned to program a VCR. When I went to college, there were no personal computers. I wrote every paper by hand and then typed them on my electric typewriter. Now, as I type this on my laptop two decades later in a home practically run by computers, I am awed by the extraordinary changes technology has brought to every aspect of my life.

In terms of technological savvy and use, I'd say I'm halfway between a traditionalist and an enthusiast—an "appreciatist"! There's no way I would have survived my daughter's first year away at college without FaceTime, but the fast pace and constant updates of technology can be intimidating. Enhancements happen in the blink of an eye, rendering the knowledge I've gained obsolete. I feel I'm always on the starting line of a new race. However, there's no denying the power of technology, particularly in the classroom.

Specifically, technology fuels my writing workshop lessons, and the impact on my students' academic experience is indelible. Seven years ago, I was one of a handful of pioneers in my school district who switched from the chalkboard to the Smart Board. Back then, my students needed to go to a shared computer lab to use a computer; they used one only to publish their writing. Now, all my students use Chromebooks at every stage of the writing process. My school's technology facilitator has become an invaluable resource. Several times a week I pick his brain for solutions to challenges I've encountered or for creative, tech-rich tips I can pass along to my students.

Writing workshop is where magic happens. Precious ideas full of promise are shared, nurtured, and celebrated. The energy and excitement are palpable. To develop their ideas, my students use Chromebooks, Google Docs, Photo Story 3 for Windows, and Movie Maker, among many other applications. I also flip my writing workshop lessons, making it possible for my students to have dynamic interactions with content, peers, and me. The efficiency with which I'm able to teach and my students are able to learn are compelling reasons to embrace flipped learning.

Definition of Flipped Learning

Flipped learning and *flipped classroom* (the terms are used synonymously) are current buzzwords in education. Entering either term in any search engine calls up articles, blogs, and Twitter postings by people sharing their successes using this pedagogical approach or asking questions about what it entails. Teachers regularly ask, "Isn't it what the kids are doing for homework?" When we first starting using flipped learning (the term we prefer because it emphasizes learning and not a physical space), we asked the same questions, so let's begin by clarifying what it is and how we define it.

Flipped learning is a pedagogical approach—a teaching method. It's a blended-learning approach to instruction. Catlin R. Tucker, author of *Blended Learning in Grades 4–12* (2012), defines blended learning as a hybrid style in which educators "combine traditional face-to-face instruction with an online component" (11). This approach promotes student-centered learning and engagement. Like every other teaching method, we use it when we believe it will help foster student learning in rich and meaningful ways. It may play a central or more minor role in the classroom.

Flipped learning has sparked conversations about the role of the teacher, the role of the student, and how students learn content (specifically, *where* and *how* direct instruction is delivered—in the classroom, at home, or both). Teachers who use flipped learning believe in the effectiveness of direct, or explicit, instruction and its benefits in the classroom. Rosenshine (1987) defines explicit instruction as a "systematic method of teaching with emphasis on proceeding in small steps, checking for student understanding, and achieving active and successful participation by all students" (34). Elements of this teaching method include presentation, guided practice, assessment and feedback, and independent practice (Archer and Hughes 2011). We believe explicit, direct instruction is an effective teaching method to use in writing workshop. Is it the only teaching method we use? No. It is one effective method for teaching, in addition to others. See Figure Intro.1 for more information about what flipped learning is and is not.

Flipped learning is . . .	Flipped learning is not . . .
› blended learning	› online tutoring
› student-centered	› one size fits all
› individualized	› only for homework
› engaging	› a lecture
› created by the teacher	› a replacement for the teacher
› interactive	› passive
› efficient	› every day, all day
› assessed	› accessible only from home
› setting and meeting goals	
› concise and to the point	
› strategies and models	
› tailored to specific instances when students need extra support or a challenge	

Flipped learning is a relatively new term and its definition is amorphous; educators, researchers, and administrators use it to label many different forms of learning, which has contributed to the tensions surrounding its use in the classroom. Troy Cockrum, author of *Flipping Your English Class to Reach All Learners* (2014), defines flipping a classroom as "using technology to deliver asynchronous direct instruction with the intention of freeing up class time for student-centered learning" (9). He notes that because there are so many interpretations of the term, the model looks different in every classroom. Bergmann and Sams, authors of *Flip Your Classroom: Reach Every Student in Every Class Every Day* (2012) and prominent advocates in the flipped classroom movement, agree; they encourage teachers to customize this teaching approach to suit the needs of their students. They note that "one unifying characteristic of all flipped classrooms is the desire to redirect the attention in the classroom away from the teacher and onto the learners and the learning" (96). In short, the goal of flipped learning is to create more time for active learning in the classroom by relocating direct instruction to other times in the day, such as after school. As a result of the scrutiny given the term's nebulous meaning, the Flipped Learning Network released a definition of flipped learning on March 12, 2014:

> Flipped learning is a pedagogical approach in which direct instruction moves from the group learning space to the individual learning space, and the resulting group space is transformed into a dynamic, interactive

learning environment where the educator guides students as they apply concepts and engage creatively in the subject matter. (http://flippedlearning.org/domain/46)

We've aligned our approach to flipped learning during writing workshop with this definition because it emphasizes shifting whole-class direct instruction to individual instruction.

Research on Flipped Learning

Despite the increased research related to online and podcast learning, there are very few studies examining flipped learning in high school, middle school, and elementary school classrooms. However, flipped learning is used in many college courses (Arnaud 2013), and research on its use in that context has identified the following benefits:

» differentiation
» engagement
» independence
» efficiency

Bergmann and Sams (2012), high school chemistry teachers in Woodland Park, Colorado, found that flipping their teaching transformed their classrooms. They saw increased differentiation and engagement because their students could work at their own pace, review material on their own, and advance their understanding of the content. Bergmann, Overmyer, and Wilie (2011) also noted a rise in student engagement. Students' motivation increased as a result of learning actively during class time and having more opportunities to interact with peers and teachers. Their students enjoyed flipped learning far more than a traditional lecture. Overall, flipped learning classrooms have the advantages of online learning (students can review concepts and select the content they need to learn) as well as the advantages of a workshop (students have a classroom space in which to ask questions of their peers and their teacher, seeking clarity and feedback).

Research also points to increased efficiency. Teachers gain back time to initiate active learning, provide feedback, and ask questions. In a study by Leicht et al. (2012) that tracked flipped learning in an engineering class, students reported that having time to work independently and being able to use technology were more effective than a traditional lecture; they felt more confident in their understanding. Leicht et al. and Talley and Scherer (2013) found increased student achievement in classrooms using flipped learning. Talley and Scherer noted that flipped learning, with its flexibility and opportunities for active learning, increased their students' understanding of the material.

All teachers are researchers. We make observations, collect data, alter our approach, and assess the results. We encourage you to try flipped learning and evaluate the results. We believe you too will find increased student differentiation, engagement, independence, and efficiency.

The Flipped Writing Workshop

Writing workshop is a natural venue in which to increase differentiation, engagement, and efficiency and promote choice and independent learning. Flipped learning dovetails with the structures already in place, which include the minilesson, small-group work, and one-on-one learning.

Drawing on the work of Lucy Calkins (1994), Nancie Atwell (1987), Fountas and Pinnell (2001), and Donald Graves (2003), we have designed our workshops in ways that prioritize active student learning and, most important, time in which to write. Fountas and Pinnell write, "The purpose of the writing workshop is to give students opportunities to write within the school day and to provide appropriate, intensive, targeted instruction to the whole group, small groups, and individuals" (50). We wanted to devote more time to student writing and individual instruction. Using flipped learning in writing workshop helped us achieve these goals.

Before we began flipping our lessons, a typical writing workshop included a minilesson, time for students to write and/or meet one-on-one with us, and last, a time to share and set goals about what they would like to work on in the future. Using flipped learning in place of some minilessons freed up time for more student writing and conferring. Lucy Calkins (1994) first envisioned the writing workshop minilesson as a brief time (five to ten minutes) in which teachers "offer something to the group that is meant to inspire and instruct" (189). Since we believe strongly in the value of minilessons in writing workshop, the idea of flipping them was initially terrifying. What would happen if we encouraged our students to learn some minilessons on their own? Would these flipped lessons be just as effective? Would students' learning suffer? How would these changes affect our writing workshop? What we found astonished us (and we think it will astonish you too). When we flipped some of our lessons, we covered more content. We had more time for individualized instruction and conferences. Our students set goals about what they needed to learn, sought out the information on their own, and had more time for writing. We rejoiced at the changes we were seeing: our students were taking more ownership of their learning and making choices about what they needed to learn.

What does flipped learning in a writing workshop look like? Imagine being able to teach a new minilesson and review three previous ones in one workshop session. All—yes, all—your students are able to set goals, have their needs addressed, and write. Additionally, you're able to confer with several students and quickly assess their progress. Here are two examples:

> You're teaching a narrative writing unit in third grade and you notice that your students have different skills they need to work on. Several need to

learn how to create paragraphs, several others are exploring strategies for elaboration, and two are ready for the challenge of writing a flashback. You send these students to their computers or tablets to find the lessons they need while you confer with others.

Or perhaps you're teaching a fifth-grade essay unit. Some of your students are ready to move on to writing counterclaims in their arguments. Some need to review how to write a thesis statement. Two need help using transitional phrases to distinguish their arguments from their counterclaims. You direct your students to flipped lessons on their tablets or computers that address their needs. Your students become more independent in their learning, and you are free to meet with more of them individually.

A writing workshop, in all its wonderfully chaotic glory, functions more smoothly and efficiently with flipped learning. We invite you to embrace flipped learning as a liberating teaching approach in elementary and middle school writing workshops that lets students work productively, at their own pace, with you there to model and guide. These lessons can then be accessed whenever students need them, including at home, which is incredibly helpful for parents who wonder, "What is my child learning? What is he being asked to do?"

Overview of This Book

Chapter 1 offers guidelines for determining which writing lessons to flip and why. We present a framework, based on five essential questions, that crystallizes the process. We discuss technology platforms, options, and resources. We also include processes for creating flipped lessons and how these lessons can be incorporated into your writing workshop. Finally, we include assessment practices to guide your evaluation of flipped learning and your students' learning.

Chapter 2 discusses the challenge of helping students generate ideas to write about. We demonstrate how flipping lessons helps students access the instruction they need when they need it.

Drafting is the focus of **Chapter 3**. We often race around the classroom during this step, trying to address many and varied needs. Flipped lessons are a way to clone ourselves, to help each student reach his or her goals.

Chapter 4 explores the challenges of getting students to perceive revision as a pivotal step in the writing process. Revising can seem daunting. Flipped lessons encourage students to practice and apply strategies that help them see their writing in a different light and make key changes that improve it.

Chapter 5 explores flipped lessons as a way to provide explicit instruction students need to strengthen the mechanics of their writing.

Chapter 6 focuses on publishing and celebrating students' writing. There are a variety of options for making students' work public and sharing it with others. Flipped lessons help students navigate these choices and make important decisions.

Chapters 2–6 include these recurring components:

» We unpack a specific step in the writing process and discuss some of the typical challenges our students face during it. We then demonstrate how flipped learning helps us anticipate challenges, address students' needs, and maximize instructional time in the writing workshop.

» We provide a snapshot of how and when we send our students off to work, including what led to the flipped lesson and what occurred after it (minilesson, small-group work, independent work, homework).

» We model a flipped lesson, including the technology used, a "top five" list of additional lessons we recommend flipping, tech tips for both novice and advanced users of technology, and brief suggestions for ways to assess students.

» We identify opportunities for reflection that help us assess our needs and help our students monitor their learning.

USING FLIPPED LEARNING IN WRITING WORKSHOP

I noticed my daughter using a lesson for her sixth-grade homework this year and was curious. I watched along with her as her teacher explained how to find reliable sources on the Internet and was amazed. What an enriching addition to classroom teaching. What an opportunity—and challenge—for my daughter to reflect independently. Most exciting for me was that I could be part of her learning—we discussed the topic together. This shared learning experience between parent and child is rare in a traditional academic setting, although it is meaningful intellectually and emotionally. I would guess the lesson was exciting for my daughter's teacher to create, and my daughter and I, in turn, felt special because she had taken the time and effort to do so. Lessons like this require much effort; teachers need to be given the time and resources to create them.

—Ms. Bennett

How often during writing workshop do we think, "If only I could clone myself!"? Whether we have fifteen students or thirty, it's challenging (and sometimes impossible) to give each one the individual support he or she needs daily. Combine this self-imposed pressure to be "super teacher" with the realities of delivering the curriculum and meeting Common Core State Standards, and we may feel we're forever walking uphill. We crave efficiency and search for ways to maximize our teaching minutes.

Lucy Calkins (1994) recommends keeping the minilesson as short as possible (it's called a *minilesson* for a reason) so students have more time to write. Flipped learning provides opportunities to remove some minilessons from the workshop, offer differentiated instruction that addresses a variety of needs, and make more time for writing during each session.

Flipping lessons doesn't have to be as time-consuming as many teachers make it out to be. Start small and think about flipping lessons that will yield the best results. We suggest you start by reflecting on your teaching and your students and jotting down answers to these questions:

What am I noticing?
What seems to be working?
What could be better?
What isn't working?
Where do I feel frustrated?
When do my students seem to be frustrated?

Then look back over the previous year. Go ahead: hit the rewind button and reflect. What instruction did you repeat again and again, unit after unit, in whole-class lessons, minilessons, and conferences? Why? Chances are these lessons are the ones students struggled with, required additional support to understand, needed more help to internalize, or forgot once they were immersed in other aspects of the writing process.

Next, determine which of these lessons can be flipped and which can't. For a variety of reasons—intricacy, the complexity of the skill being taught, the momentum and enthusiasm the concept requires—some lessons *must* be taught in the classroom. You also need to consider what is best for your students; many lessons are *better* taught in the classroom. However, lessons you need to reteach throughout the year are great ones to flip, as are the ones you don't have time to get to.

Your list of flippable lessons may still be long, but to make the best use of your instructional time and keep the process manageable (We're talking to you, "super teacher"!), choose just five to start with. (Our list is shown in Figure 1.1.) Once you get the hang of the process and try out some flipped lessons with your students, you can determine their effectiveness, make changes, and flip additional lessons. (In the upcoming chapters, we identify five lessons with flip potential for each step of the writing process.)

A Framework for Flipping Writing Workshop Lessons

You're now ready to decide how you will flip these lessons. Based on the research we conducted in our writing workshops; the literature on flipped learning; and our thinking before, during, and after creating flipped lessons, we developed a framework delineating the steps in creating effective, engaging flipped lessons that will meet students' needs (see Figure 1.2). (You can use the related blank organizer in the Appendix to plan individual lessons.) The framework's components are discussed in depth in the following sections.

FIGURE 1.2 ▼
Framework for
Flipping Lessons

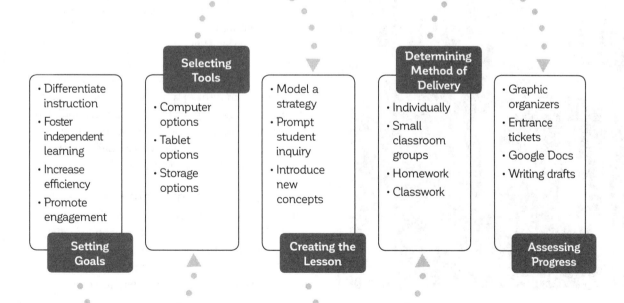

- Differentiate instruction
- Foster independent learning
- Increase efficiency
- Promote engagement

Setting Goals

Selecting Tools

- Computer options
- Tablet options
- Storage options

- Model a strategy
- Prompt student inquiry
- Introduce new concepts

Creating the Lesson

Determining Method of Delivery

- Individually
- Small classroom groups
- Homework
- Classwork

- Graphic organizers
- Entrance tickets
- Google Docs
- Writing drafts

Assessing Progress

Setting Goals: Why Do I Want to Flip This Lesson?

Begin by asking yourself, "Why am I flipping *this* lesson?" There are many reasons to flip a lesson. Perhaps you find yourself teaching the lesson over and over during the year, so your goal is efficiency. Or, if you're looking for ways to increase student choice, your goals might be differentiation and engagement. Four purposes, discussed in the following sections, best encompass the reasons for flipping a lesson.

Differentiate Instruction

An essential component of writing workshop is differentiating instruction to meet the needs of all learners. Tomlinson and Imbeau (2010) define differentiation as

"a philosophy—a way of thinking about teaching and learning" (13). Key elements of differentiated instruction include understanding students as unique learners with strengths, affinities, and challenges; planning and targeting instruction to meet the many different needs of students; and maintaining a flexible approach to teaching by asking, "What does *this* student need at *this* moment?" (14). Questions to ask related to differentiation are *How is this lesson going to meet the needs of my students? Which students in my classroom will benefit from this lesson?*

We've all had the experience where our students in a writing workshop were at different places, each working on their own writing at their own pace. We love the gentle, chaotic hum. This is how learning best takes place. However, when assessing our students' work, we may notice that several students could benefit from reviewing lessons taught the previous week, month, or year. We might also notice students who need to deepen their understanding of a concept. Instead of teaching each student one-on-one in a writing conference, we can differentiate our teaching through flipped learning.

Foster Independent Learning

All teachers dream of fostering a writing workshop in which students own their learning, independently setting goals and solving them. Troy Hicks (2009) describes how technology can provide opportunities for students to become independent learners:

If we engage students in real writing tasks and we use technology in such a way that it complements their innate need to find purposes and audiences for their work, we can have them engaged in a digital writing process that focuses first on the writer, then on the writing, and lastly on the technology. (8)

Using flipped learning, students can set their own goals and decide which information they need. With access to a digital library of flipped lessons, they can personalize their learning by deciding which concepts they need to learn, review, or deepen. They can set goals at the start of the workshop, midway through, or at the end, perhaps jotting them down on a sticky note (see Figure 1.3) or in their writing notebook.

FIGURE 1.3 ▼
Sticky Note

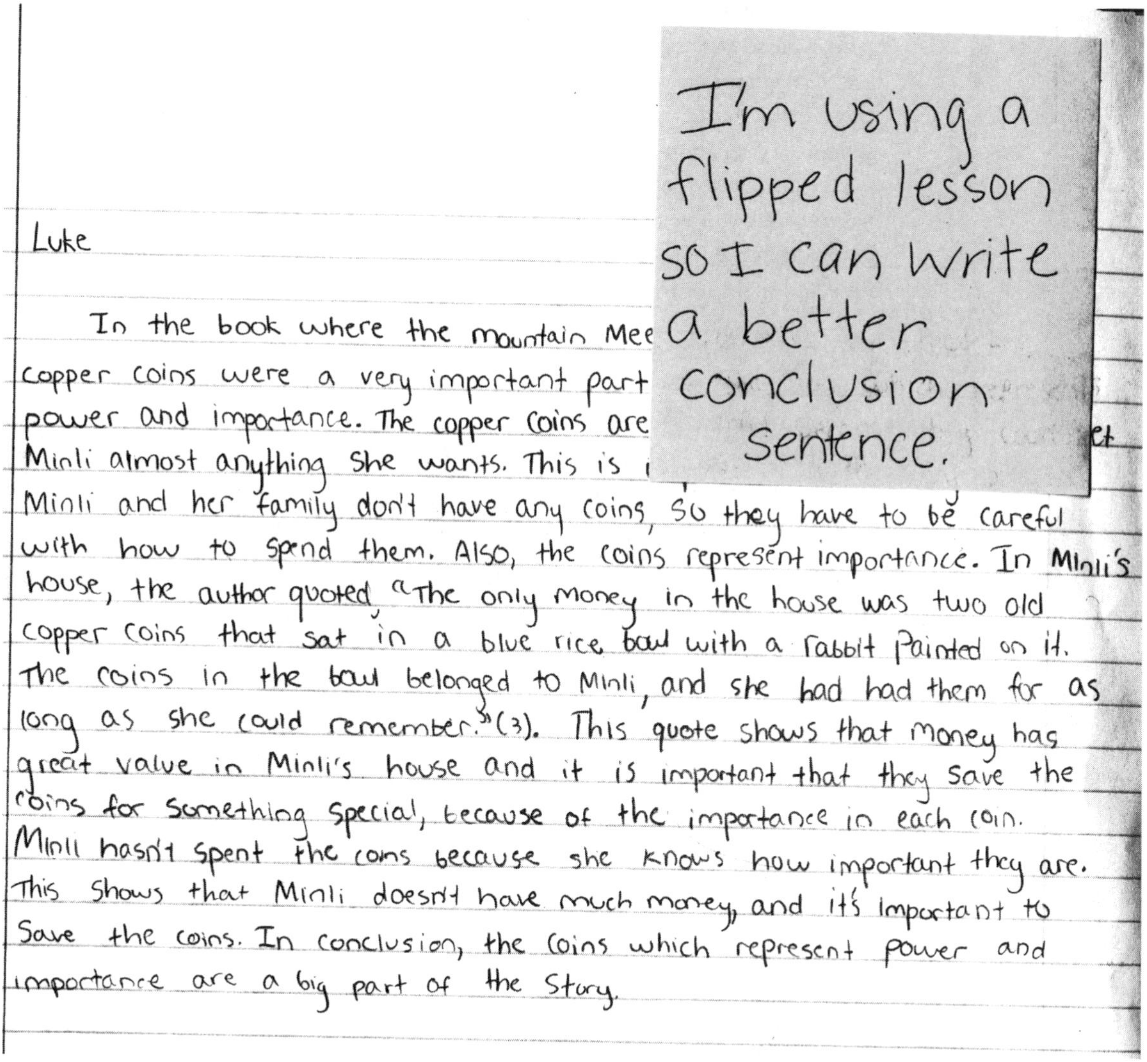

Luke

In the book where the mountain Mee [I'm using a flipped lesson so I can write a better conclusion sentence.] copper coins were a very important part [of] power and importance. The copper coins are [money and] Minli almost anything she wants. This is [because] Minli and her family don't have any coins, so they have to be careful with how to spend them. Also, the coins represent importance. In Minli's house, the author quoted "The only money in the house was two old copper coins that sat in a blue rice bowl with a rabbit painted on it. The coins in the bowl belonged to Minli, and she had had them for as long as she could remember." (3). This quote shows that money has great value in Minli's house and it is important that they save the coins for something special, because of the importance in each coin. Minli hasn't spent the coins because she knows how important they are. This shows that Minli doesn't have much money, and it's important to save the coins. In conclusion, the coins which represent power and importance are a big part of the story.

We've all used exit tickets to assess student learning, but with flipped learning, Bergmann and Sams (2012) recommend using an entrance ticket (see Figure 1.4) to help students outline their goals at the beginning of a workshop session. Students write down a recent flipped lesson that helped them improve their writing and to which they would like to refer during the session. Although students are generally good about budgeting the time they spend with flipped lessons, it's a good idea to limit them to one or two per session. That way, they can get to what really matters—writing.

Increase Efficiency

Time flies; it is precious and scarce. One of the biggest benefits of flipped learning is the gift of time. You no longer need to review and reteach concepts through whole-class lessons. Instead, you flip lessons your students can review throughout the year whenever they need to. Lessons you reteach each year probably include those on writing dialogue, how to generate topics for writing, and the concluding sentence of a paragraph, to name just a few.

Using flipped lessons also increases the content you can cover. You probably have lessons you wish you could teach but never have the time for or a whole unit you would love to teach but can't fit into the curriculum. Flipped learning provides time and space for this, and students' writing skills improve accordingly.

Promote Engagement

Increasing motivation and student engagement is a benefit frequently noted in research related to flipped learning, one linked to opportunities for increased ownership, pace, and choice. Students enjoy learning from short, creative, attention-grabbing lessons at times of their choosing and in locations where they learn best (such as quiet study areas instead of a noisy classroom).

Whether you are looking to differentiate instruction, foster independent learning, increase efficiency, or promote engagement, it is important to identify your primary purpose for creating flipped learning lessons.

FIGURE 1.4 ▼
Flipped Lesson
Entrance Ticket

Flipped Lesson Entrance Ticket

Lesson Topic: _____

Based on this lesson, what is your understanding of _____ ?

_____

_____

_____

Name one strategy you've learned and believe will help you with your writing:

_____

Have you applied this strategy to your writing yet?

_____ Yes   _____ No

If yes, how?

_____

_____

If no, why? Should this be part of your writing goals today?

_____

_____

_____

_____

_____

_____

Selecting Tools: How Am I Going to Flip This Lesson?

For teachers new to flipped learning, selecting tools can create a great deal of anxiety. Use what you're comfortable with; don't become bogged down and intimidated. When you're overwhelmed, it's easy to quit before you start. Review the goals of your lesson and choose familiar tools that are easy to use.

Surfing the Internet for flipped lessons will turn up numerous award-winning examples. Don't let them intimidate you. Every teacher can create effective, instructional lessons using tools she or he is comfortable with and has access to. And although you may be tempted to take a why-reinvent-the-wheel approach and use flipped lessons someone else has created, you shouldn't. Your students will learn best from lessons that feature your face or voice. They want to see and hear *you*!

The most popular technology or software option for flipping a lesson is a screencast—a recording of what is shown on your computer or tablet screen. Students hear your voice thinking aloud and explaining but see only what is on the screen. There are many computer software options and tablet apps, a few of which are discussed in the following sections.

Screencast Options for Computers

» **Camtasia ($$$).** This software creates screencasts with all the bells and whistles you dream of. We give it an "advanced user" ranking, for teachers who are quite comfortable using more complex technology tools. Unless your school has a subscription, it will cost you more than one hundred dollars to purchase. (Chapter 5 has an example.)

» **Screencastify (free).** This Google Drive app is an easy solution for filming your flipped lessons. Download Screencastify from the Google app store, and it will immediately appear in your Chrome toolbar. Simply click on the icon and begin recording. The best part about using this Google tool is that all your flipped lessons will be saved instantly in your Google Drive account. Share the lesson with students just as you would a Google Doc. You can also create a shared Google folder and create a collection of Screencastify lessons that your students can access.

» **Screencast-O-Matic (free).** This is a very user-friendly, flexible option for novices. It captures what you do in Word, PowerPoint, Keynote, or Prezi. (Chapter 2 has an example.)

» **Smart Notebook ($$).** Interactive whiteboards can also be used to record screencasts. We create presentations using our Smart Notebook software, record the lesson using the interactive whiteboard, and save it as a screencast. This software will automatically create a QuickTime movie for you to upload to a website or store on a flash drive. (Chapter 4 has an example of a lesson created using Smart Notebook.)

Screencast Options for Tablets

Some schools now provide every student with a tablet; if yours does, creating screencasts of flipped lessons on a tablet will have great appeal. Here are a few apps for doing so (while many are free, they may limit your ability to upload the files to a secure website easily):

» **Educreations (free).** Many teachers have their students use this free app to record their work and explain their thinking; it's quite versatile. You must create a username and password to upload lessons to the Educreations website, but with an access code, students will have instant access to your lessons.

» **Explain Everything (free).** Uploading the screencasts to YouTube, Dropbox, or Evernote is easy using this app. (Chapter 6 has an example of a lesson created using Explain Everything.)

» **ShowMe (free).** Similar to Explain Everything and Educreations, this has features that are user-friendly, especially for beginners. Like Educreations, ShowMe has a secure website to which you can upload lessons.

» **ScreenChomp, Ask3, PowToon, and Nearpod.** These additional apps are also worth checking out.

Options for Storing Flipped Lessons

Use caution when uploading lessons for elementary or middle school students to YouTube or Facebook. These media can expose students to advertisements and inappropriate content, and decisions about using social media are best made at home. In addition, many social media sites require users to be at least thirteen years old. TeacherTube and Vimeo are great alternatives; they're free and provide a safer environment for students. Google Drive, Canvas, Moodle, and other learning platforms are also becoming more commonplace in elementary and middle school classrooms. We've found these spaces to be safe and easily accessible. You could also create your own website; WordPress and Weebly are two user-friendly platforms students can safely access without advertising insertions and pop-ups. Still another alternative is to use flash drives in the classroom and lend them to students for individual use.

If you have questions about where best to store your flipped lessons, speak to a member of your tech support staff or to colleagues who have created Internet content. You may also tweet us at @LitLearnAct; we welcome any questions or comments.

CREATING THE LESSON | How Will I Structure This Lesson? Which Teaching Approach Will I Use?

Now that you've thought through the initial steps for making your flipped lesson, it is time to create it! So what goes in the lesson? Here are some suggestions to help you structure your lesson:

1. In your first presentation slide, identify the skill or strategy you are teaching.
2. In your second presentation slide, state the learning objectives: What will students learn?
3. In slides 3–5, unpack the elements of the skill or strategy and model it.
4. Give students time to practice the skill or strategy.
5. On the final slide, encourage students to self-assess their understanding of the strategy or skill. What further steps should they take, if any?

Access the QR Code on this page (Figure 1.5) for our flipped lesson called "Creating a Flipped Lesson." This QR Code will also appear in subsequent chapters for you to reference.

There are three major approaches for teaching writing workshop concepts. Although these approaches intersect and overlap, we discuss them individually here.

FIGURE 1.5 ▲
QR Code for "Creating a Flipped Lesson"

Modeling a Strategy

With the modeling approach, you create a short, focused lesson in which you demonstrate the cognitive steps involved in some aspect of the writing process in order to help students overcome difficulties they are experiencing. Students observe an experienced writer, you, as you share authentic explanations about the writing decisions you're making, and can then try the strategy themselves.

For example, if your goal is to help students generate ideas to write about, you might think aloud as you use the photos, quotations, and jottings in your writing notebook to create a list of ideas you'll be able to return to again and again. Or, to help students include dialogue in their writing, you might verbalize your thought process as you decide what a character will say and how he or she will say it.

Prompting Student Inquiry

Inquiry-based flipped learning lessons are pegged to student-generated questions that arise during writing workshop. They encourage students to become active researchers and writers. With this approach, you build in time for students to ask questions, explore, investigate, and initiate dialogue with their peers and you. For example, to help students revise their work, you might create lessons that prompt students to reflect on the main idea in their writing, what they've discovered about themselves as a writer, and what they plan to carry over to the next writing unit.

Introducing New Concepts

Providing students with the instruction they need when they need it includes helping students who are ready for new content. For example, during a personal narrative writing unit, students who are ready to explore new literary devices can access a flipped lesson on writing a flashback or creating an allegory.

Determining the Method of Delivery: When and Where Will Students Use This Lesson?

When incorporating flipped learning lessons in your writing workshop, it is important to think about when (time of day) and where (physical space) these lessons will take place. You have multiple options for *when* and *where*. Many people think flipped learning takes place only at home, but it occurs in the classroom as well. The defining criterion is "an individual learning space." When choosing between the options, evaluate which is better case by case.

Individually in the Classroom

The best and worst aspects of writing workshop are that students work at their own pace, in different stages of the writing process, and need to learn different skills and strategies. This can engender incredible growth and creativity but at the same time can be difficult to manage. Flipped lessons help you accomplish all you can during a writing workshop because they let students manage their own learning. Within the seeming chaos, students set their own goals, recognize what they need to work on, and choose the specific lessons that will help them. They can review a concept or move on to a new challenge.

For example, perhaps your students are learning to write feature articles. You've discovered that many of them are in different stages of the process and have a variety of needs. Once you've accumulated a suite of flipped lessons, you are able to provide individual instruction to multiple students all in one writing workshop session! While one student absorbs a flipped lesson on finding an angle, another accesses a lesson on subtitles, and still another learns how to write a lead. Each student has access to what she or he needs when it's needed. (As you accumulate more flipped lessons over time, your workshop will run ever more efficiently.)

In Small Classroom Groups

When you assess your students' writing, you'll often identify three or four students who need to review the same strategy. In a perfect writing workshop, you'd have enough time to meet with the whole class, confer one-on-one with some students, and meet with small groups of students who need to work on the same writing skill. This just isn't always possible, and it can be really hard to do. Teaching students in small groups is important. These groups are not fixed, homogeneous, or grouped by ability; they are in constant flux depending on the needs of our students. Flipped learning helps you manage small-group work and reach more learners. These students can access the appropriate flipped lesson, ask questions of one another (and of you), and then try the strategy.

For example, you notice four students who are struggling with transition words in their writing. You have them gather and access a flipped lesson on transition words. Afterward, they share and peer-check their writing with one another. You follow up later with a quick check-in.

As Homework

The last option lets students review or learn a concept at home. Be sure you keep your purpose in mind and share this goal with your students. You might want students to reflect on a lesson you taught in class or you might notice some students are ready to move on. Finally, you might want to save classroom time so you can cover more content. An added benefit is the home-school partnership that develops. Parents and tutors who have access to students' lessons can be better guides. Making flipped lessons assigned as homework as interactive as possible fosters understanding. It's a good idea to include an accompanying assignment like taking notes, answering questions, or attempting the strategy or technique being learned.

Assessing Progress: How Will I Know What My Students Have Learned?

We need to know whether students have grasped the instruction we've designed. (We can't just "flip it and forget it"!) Having students complete an accompanying assignment is a common way to find out. This can take many forms:

- » summarizing the lesson using a graphic organizer
- » highlighting the section of their writing in which they plan to try out the strategy
- » completing an entrance ticket (see Figure 1.4)

Assessing flipped lessons is ongoing and iterative, so it's important to use a variety of ways to examine students' learning. Subsequent chapters provide examples of ways to assess students during specific steps of the writing process.

Working with Limited Technology?

Technology is central to flipped learning, and access can be challenging, especially in the primary grades. One way our approach to flipped learning is distinct is that it is used in the classroom as well as for homework. You may be sharing a technology lab, a laptop cart, or tablets with many other teachers and students. Student access to technology outside the classroom may also be problematic. They need to able to access the lessons assigned as homework. The reality is that students in primary and middle schools don't always have access to the technology they need.

Here are some possible solutions:

1. Make lessons generally available, as soon as and for as long as you can. This gives students who need to share technology more time.
2. Provide time to access flipped writing workshop lessons elsewhere in the day: during study hall, first thing in the morning, right after school.
3. Let students access some flipped lessons during writing workshop.
4. Lend flash drives to students who don't have access to the Internet at home.
5. Allow students to borrow tablets overnight.

Above all, be flexible. Flipped lessons are most successful when students aren't worried about being able to access them. If you set aside some writing workshop time for them and make school-provided technology available before and after regular school hours, students will be more at ease.

Flipped learning in the writing workshop shifts the power dynamic between teachers and students. Rather than waiting for teachers to review concepts or explain next steps, students are empowered to set and achieve their writing goals.

Reflecting: How Can Flipped Learning Help Me in Writing Workshop?

Wouldn't it be great if there were two or three of us in the classroom each day? Then we could accomplish all we hope to. We could observe our students more, confer with them more often, run small groups more effectively, and help our students review or learn new concepts even when they are at home. Flipped learning helps make this possible. Take some time to think about the following questions as you begin to use flipped lessons in your writing workshop.

1. How can flipped learning help me address the wide variety of needs my students have in writing workshop?
2. What is my vision for using flipped learning in the classroom—small-group work? individualized learning? both?
3. What are the lessons I find myself repeating throughout my writing workshop units? How can flipped learning help me?
4. How can I use flipped learning to increase student engagement and self-efficacy in my writing workshop?

Responses to these initial questions can inform the type of instruction we envision happening in our writing workshops. Flipped learning can help bring this vision to reality.

2

Generating Writing: Conquering the Blank Page

I did the flipped lesson last night and got some good information. I like that my teacher explains the concept with lots of examples. I also like hearing her be funny. I laugh while I'm learning.

—Eva, fourth grader

It is one week since you started a new writing unit in your classroom. All writing notebooks are decorated, and students share their works of art with pride.

"I put in this picture of me and my brother at the beach in Maine. We go there every summer," says Greg.

"These are tickets to see the Mets. I love baseball!" Maya exclaims.

"I really love elephants, so I put this picture on my notebook to show that," Meg explains.

On the pages of their notebooks, students jot down favorite words, phrases, and sentences. Lists reveal expertise around a variety of topics, favorite hobbies, and "I wonder about . . ." ideas. You are confident these initial seeds will grow into the narratives, essays, poems, and short stories your students will write this year.

The first few weeks are filled with excitement as students admire one another's notebooks and devour the mentor texts you've carefully selected to read aloud. The room hums with energy; it seems every student has ideas to contribute. Discussions flow between writing partners about books they love, techniques they can't wait to try, and the ideas they have for filling the pages of their notebooks.

With a clipboard containing an observation grid in hand, you make your way around the room, recording each student's ideas. Your goal is to confer with five or six students a day. At that pace, you'll have conferred with each student in the class by the end of the week. As students settle down and start writing, you feel good about the work that has led up to this moment and the work that will follow. "Writers, find a place to work for the next twenty minutes."

Silence envelops the room. You take this as an encouraging sign; your students must be immersed in their writing. But then you notice that while several students' hands are flying across the page, many students' hands are not. James leaves his seat to sharpen his pencil. Twice! Cynthia signs out to go to the bathroom. Maya and Sarah are looking out the window. Tammy is watching you watch her. Shayna is fidgeting. Jason and Aaron are chatting—and it isn't about their writing. What is happening? Not wanting to disrupt the silence and interrupt those who are writing, you move stealthily around the room, trying to redirect those who aren't on track. Your conference plans go out the window as you try frantically to reach each student who seems stuck. Your goal is for each student to write today, and time is running out.

Setting Goals: Why Do I Want to Flip This Lesson?

We begin each unit in writing workshop in ways we hope will inspire our students and get them revved up for writing. With great excitement, we invite our students to enter a world where their ideas are golden. Inevitably, some of them look at peers writing furiously, sigh with frustration, and proclaim, "I don't know what to write about." For them, generating ideas is intimidating and mystifying. Others eagerly fill up page after page in their notebooks and declare, "I'm finished," before some students have even begun. Anticipating this typical behavior and preparing for it by flipping a key lesson or two will help you manage your workshop more effectively and create more time for focused, purposeful, one-on-one instruction. Choose lessons that will help you throughout the year, ones students can refer to over and over. (See the decision table in Figure 2.1.)

You notice students who . . .	Your goal is for them to . . .	You create a flipped lesson . . .
are having difficulty coming up with ideas	use the strategies you taught in class to come up with ideas independently	on generating ideas that students can review (and try out) as needed
immediately have many ideas and want to move on	write a notebook entry about one idea and decide whether it is juicy enough to sustain their writing	that offers three tips for writing a juicy notebook entry, along with an example
are ready to storyboard, or outline, an idea	storyboard their idea independently	on storyboarding
do not refer to the anchor charts or their notes on generating ideas	independently use classroom anchor charts and their notes to look back at strategies for generating ideas	that introduces an interactive checklist that prompts students to refer to anchor charts and their notes

FIGURE 2.1 ▲
Decision Table for
Flipping Lessons on
Generating Ideas

Our first goal as teachers is to meet the needs of every learner in our class-room. In our writing workshop, we want to provide individualized instruction and support for all writers. A new writing unit means a fresh start and new beginning for each writer. However, it does not mean that every student starts in the same place. So we ask ourselves, *How am I ensuring that students who need to move forward can?* And *How am I helping students who need more time and practice?*

We find that a lesson on generating ideas to write about is especially helpful. Our students use this lesson over and over, whenever they've run out of ideas or need something fresh to write about. Therefore, we've used it as the model lesson for this chapter.

Selecting Tools: How Am I Going to Flip This Lesson?

We know what you're thinking. You're starting to panic about the technology. But we promise that every teacher can use flipped learning in ways with which she or he is comfortable. Use the Selecting Tools checklist in Figure 2.2 to help you decide.

Each time you create a new flipped lesson, you need to think about which tools will work for you. Time is precious. You have papers to read, meetings to attend, and lessons to plan. You need to work with tools you feel comfortable using and to which you have access, or the lesson won't happen.

The model lesson stems from the completed checklist in Figure 2.3. If you need advice, scan the QR Code in Figure 2.4 to access a flipped lesson that provides some tips. Figure 2.5 lists some strategies for using Google Slides.

> *Time is precious. You have papers to read, meetings to attend, and lessons to plan. You need to work with tools you feel comfortable using and to which you have access, or the lesson won't happen.*
>
> —Dana and Sonja

FIGURE 2.2 ▾
Selecting Tools Checklist

Selecting Tools Checklist

Flipped Lesson Topic: _____

_____

What will students learn in this lesson?

I will create my lesson using:

____ PowerPoint   ____ Word

____ Google software   ____ Other: _____

____ Interactive whiteboard software

I will record my lesson using:

____ Camtasia   ____ Tablet app

____ Screencast-O-Matic   ____ Other: _____

____ Cell phone

I will upload my lesson to:

____ YouTube   ____ Google Classroom

____ Vimeo   ____ Class website/platform

____ TeacherTube   ____ Zaption

____ Tablet app website   ____ Other: _____

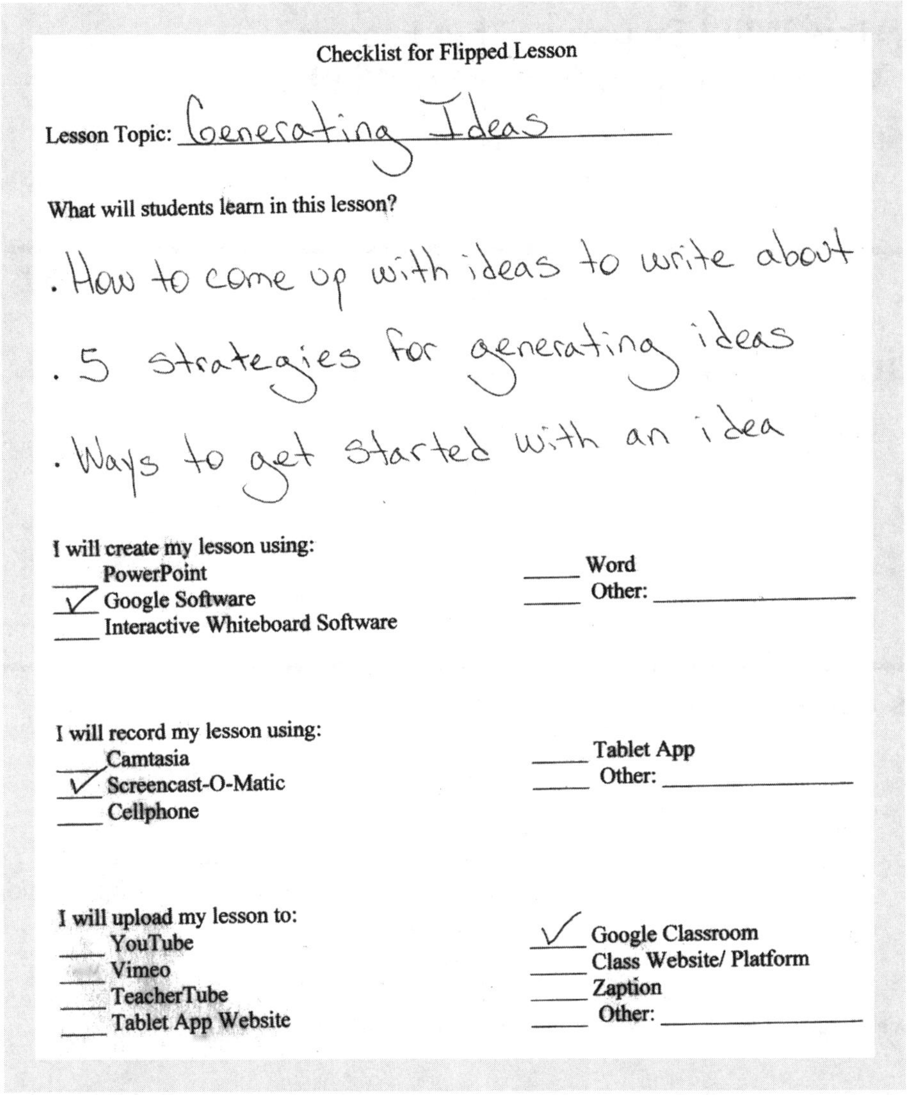

Checklist for Flipped Lesson

Lesson Topic: _Generating Ideas_

What will students learn in this lesson?

- How to come up with ideas to write about
- 5 strategies for generating ideas
- Ways to get started with an idea

I will create my lesson using:
- _____ PowerPoint
- _✓_ Google Software
- _____ Interactive Whiteboard Software
- _____ Word
- _____ Other: _____

I will record my lesson using:
- _____ Camtasia
- _✓_ Screencast-O-Matic
- _____ Cellphone
- _____ Tablet App
- _____ Other: _____

I will upload my lesson to:
- _____ YouTube
- _____ Vimeo
- _____ TeacherTube
- _____ Tablet App Website
- _✓_ Google Classroom
- _____ Class Website/ Platform
- _____ Zaption
- _____ Other: _____

FIGURE 2.4 ▲
QR Code for "Creating
a Flipped Lesson"

TECH**TIP** Google Slides is similar to PowerPoint or Keynote. When using Google Slides, choose a template that is clean and uncluttered. Use Google Slides' animation features. They will help engage your learners. You can also use Google's screencasting app, Screencastify, to record your presentation in Google Slides.

CREATING THE LESSON | How Will I Structure This Lesson? Which Teaching Approach Will I Use?

For this lesson we used Google Slides (always use fewer than ten slides; the pace needs to be quick and focused). See Figure 2.6 for snapshots from the flipped lesson.

Generating Ideas
Conquering The Blank Page!

▲ **FIGURE 2.6 a** Lesson Topic

Objectives:
- Learning where ideas come from
- Strategies for coming up with ideas to write about
- Getting started!

▲ **FIGURE 2.6 b** Learning Objectives

Where do ideas come from?
- Family
- Pets
- Nature
- Vacations
- Holidays
- Traditions
- Special objects
- Food
- Sports
- Emotions

▲ **FIGURE 2.6 c** Content—Model Process of Brainstorming

You Try!

List 3 ideas you can write about:

1) Going to the movies with Eddie
2) Mia swiping a granola bar off the kitchen counter!
3) Autumn

▲ **FIGURE 2.6 d** Content—Think Aloud

Getting Started!

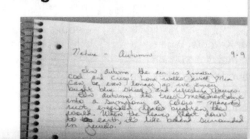

▲ **FIGURE 2.6 e** Write Aloud. Then, Students Try!

How'd You Do?

- Reflect on your learning. Were you able to get started with an idea?
- What questions do you have?
- Be prepared to share your work with me when we conference.

▲ **FIGURE 2.6 f** Assessment—Students Self-Assess Their Work and Understanding

COMMENTS/INSTRUCTIONS

Dear Shawn,

Enclosed is a complimentary copy of Flip Your Writing Workshop, for which you provided composition services.

I included extras so you'd have the photo of your grandson and his friend, too, in case you want to send to them.

Thank you again! It's a beauty!!

Signed:

The teaching approach is modeling strategies: To make the process of generating ideas visible and provide concrete strategies, Sonja *thinks* and *writes* aloud. She models how the photos and quotes she used to decorate her notebook cover spark ideas to write about. She models how creating a list of ideas based on the people, places, and things she loves helps her start writing. She then asks students to try out each of these strategies in their writing notebook. The lesson is short and focused and includes several options for getting started from which students can choose.

Sonja filmed the lesson using the screencast software Screencast-O-Matic. Google Slides and Screencast-O-Matic remained our go-to choices for a long time. Screencast-O-Matic is free, is easy to use, and has editing features. (See Figure 2.7 for some pros and cons of working with these tools.) Once we grew more comfortable with creating flipped lessons, we tried screencasting tools such as Camtasia, which include more bells and whistles.

You can access this lesson by scanning the QR Code in Figure 2.8. It includes an example of the work a student produced after the lesson.

	Pros	Cons
Google Slides	<ul><li>Free!</li><li>Very easy to use</li><li>Simple, clean layouts</li><li>Includes animation</li><li>Stores easily on Google Drive</li><li>Students can be part of the presentation</li><li>Has free tutorials</li></ul>	<ul><li>Limited backgrounds</li><li>Limited features</li></ul>
Screencast-O-Matic	<ul><li>Free!</li><li>Easy to download</li><li>Easy to use</li><li>Has free tutorials</li><li>Allows editing</li><li>Resulting lessons are easy to download</li><li>Easy to upload lessons to sites like YouTube, Vimeo, and TeacherTube</li></ul>	<ul><li>Limited features</li><li>Limited editing options</li><li>No animation</li><li>No bells and whistles</li></ul>

◄ FIGURE 2.7
Pros and Cons of Google Slides and Screencast-O-Matic

FIGURE 2.8 ▲
QR Code for Sample Lesson

Determining the Method of Delivery: When and Where Will Students Use This Lesson?

The lesson is ready to use. But how? How will it help you individualize instruction for your students? Flipped lessons are not just homework; you have choices about when and where to use them (see Figure 2.9). For example, you might assign this lesson to a small group of students who need additional practice with generating ideas. Or you might assign it as homework and have students bring in their ideas the next day.

Sonja often uses this flipped lesson in her writing workshop. One day she gathers her writers together on the rug, their writing notebooks and pencils in hand, and presents a whole-class minilesson quickly reviewing previously taught strategies for generating ideas and then teaching a new one. She adds the new strategy to the classroom anchor chart and has her students begin generating ideas.

As she circles the room, she notices two students who are having trouble coming up with ideas. Talking with them for a few minutes reveals that they need a different plan of action. She recommends that they try the strategy they learned today and if that doesn't help that they access the flipped lesson. Having suggested two paths, she hopes they will independently decide what they need. She tells them she'll touch base with them in ten minutes and check their progress.

Continuing to circle the room, she meets with some students who are eager to get started writing entries. She offers a few quick tips, and they get started. Glancing at the two students who were having difficulty, she sees they are using the flipped lesson together and jotting down ideas. She feels victorious! It's a small step but an important one. These students have made a plan and are seeking further information independently. The flipped lesson is helping them review strategies and move forward in their writing.

When Sonja touches base with them a bit later, she compliments their hard work and initiative and asks which strategy worked best for them. At the end of the workshop, she asks all her students to share the strategy that helped them generate ideas. The students who accessed the flipped lesson eagerly share a strategy they reviewed there.

FIGURE 2.9 ▶
Flipped Lessons Aren't
Just Homework!

Here are five ways you can use this lesson in your classroom:

1. With a small group or partnership
2. During a one-on-one conference
3. With a student working independently
4. As homework
5. Anytime!

At the end of the day, Sonja reflects on the workshop. The flipped lesson worked and is ready to be used the next day should another student need it. Helping two students conquer the blank page is a small step. But it's a mighty step in the lives of those two writers.

Creating a Formative Assessment: How Will I Know What My Students Have Learned?

Determining what and how well our students learn is a daily concern. Assessment is a hot-button issue in education, something we grapple with constantly, and it isn't limited to lengthy summative assessments. The formative assessments we conduct in our classrooms each day inform our teaching and help us determine best practices. Formative assessments also help students monitor their own progress and decide when they need support, when they're ready for new challenges. This is at the heart of flipped learning—a focus on the quality rather than the quantity of the work students produce.

Students appreciate clear, structured routines that expect them to engage in active learning. You and your students can assess the success of flipped lessons if you establish and conduct routine reflection and goal setting:

1. Provide guidelines. If you limit students' use of flipped lessons to one a day, they'll be able to spend the majority of the workshop writing.
2. Share your expectations for how students will respond and reflect on their flipped learning. Where will they take notes? Where will they try out the strategies they learn?
3. Establish a goal-setting routine, either right after the minilesson or at the end of the workshop.

One way you can assess the usefulness of your flipped lessons in writing workshop is to review the notes students take during the flipped lessons and the writing they do as a result. Teachers new to flipped learning often wonder, "What are the students doing during flipped lessons? Are they just sitting there watching the screen? Are they passive?" Flipped lessons are *not* passive; they are interactive. During the lesson, students take notes in their writing notebooks, try out new strategies in their writing, set goals, and reflect on what they understand and what questions they still have. Whether your students are third graders, fifth graders, or eighth graders, flipped lessons need to include interactive components that help you assess your students' understanding of the material.

Figure 2.10 shows some of the notes a student has taken as she accessed this model flipped lesson. Students of any age can do this work. Figure 2.11 provides tips related to taking notes during a flipped lesson, trying out writing strategies, and setting goals. If students take notes on and try out the strategies they are taught, they write more confidently.

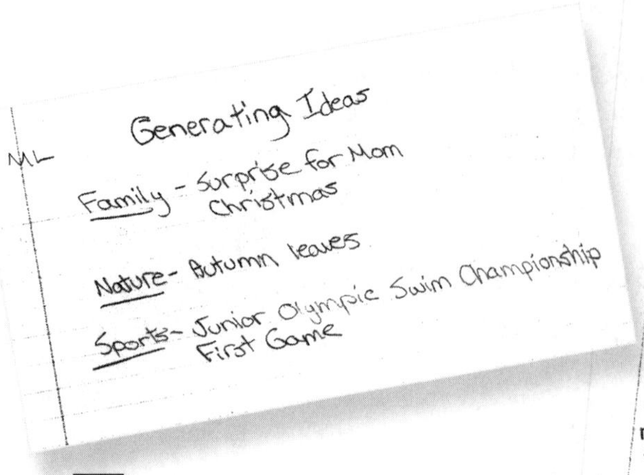

ML

Generating Ideas

Family - Surprise for Mom
Christmas

Nature - Autumn leaves

Sports - Junior Olympic Swim Championship
First Game

a

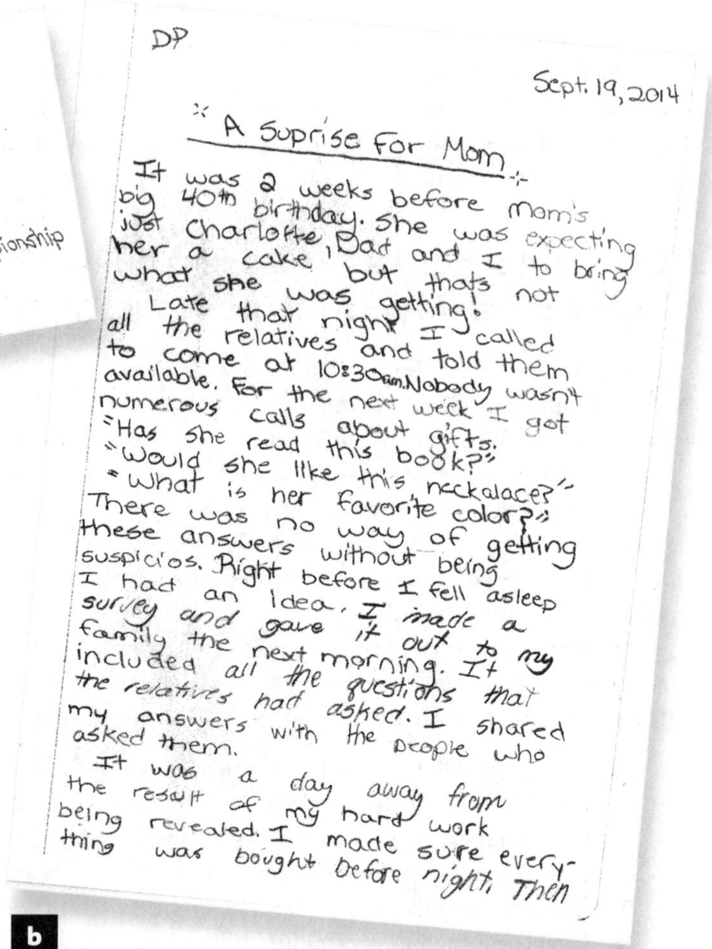

DP

Sept. 19, 2014

A Suprise For Mom

It was 2 weeks before Mom's big 40th birthday. She was expecting just Charlotte, Dad and I to bring her a cake, but thats not what she was getting!

Late that night I called all the relatives and told them to come at 10:30am. Nobody wasn't available. For the next week I got numerous calls about gifts.
"Has she read this book?"
"Would she like this neckalace?"
"What is her favorite color?"
There was no way of getting these answers without being suspicios. Right before I fell asleep I had an idea. I made a survey and gave it out to my family the next morning. It included all the questions that the relatives had asked. I shared my answers with the people who asked them.

It was a day away from the result of my hard work being revealed. I made sure every-thing was bought before night. Then

b

FIGURE 2.10 ▸

a Student Trying Out Flipped Lesson Strategies

b Student Implementing a Strategy and Writing

FIGURE 2.11 ▸
Tips Regarding Formative Assessment

- At the beginning of each flipped lesson, state clearly the materials and supplies students need to get ready. ("You will need your writing notebook, a pencil, and two sticky notes.")
- Be clear and direct about what students will write down and where their notes should go. ("All of your flipped lesson notes today will go on the next blank page in your writing notebook.")
- Pause when you want students to take notes or try a strategy. State your directions clearly. ("Pause here and write down the notes." "Stop here and try this strategy in your notebook.")
- Ask students to set goals or reflect. ("At this time, I'd like you to pause and reflect on the strategies taught in this lesson. Write down what is going well and what questions you have.")
- Above all, encourage students to write down their questions during the lesson so they can ask them in a conference.

Top Five Flipped Lessons for Generating Ideas

Students benefit from any number of lessons about generating ideas to write about, in both fiction and nonfiction. In addition to this model lesson—"Generating Ideas"—we've had great success with the following:

- » Role of a Writing Partner
- » Storyboarding
- » Outlining an Essay
- » Creating a Character
- » Writing a Thesis Statement

We teach these lessons again and again during a school year. Flipping them helps us run smoother writing workshops and maximize our time in the classroom. Anticipating the needs of our students, we flip lessons that provide the greatest return on our investment and help increase classroom efficiency.

Final Reflection

Reflecting on flipped learning, like the process of writing, is iterative. At this point, you've created at least one flipped lesson for generating ideas. Before moving on to the next chapter, think deeply about flipped lessons during the generating phase. Jot down your responses to these four questions in your teacher journal:

1. In what ways did flipped learning increase independence and engagement in the generating phase of writing?
2. Which flipped lessons were most effective at helping students come up with ideas to write about?
3. Did the flipped lessons help students learn strategies to overcome writing blocks?
4. In which ways did flipped learning help me differentiate my instruction?

Your responses to these questions can raise awareness about the difference flipped lessons make during the generating phase. Such focus can inform your instruction and prompt future flipped lessons.

DRAFTING:
WRITING WITH INTENT

The thing about the flipped lessons in writing workshop is that I am interacting with them. I prefer to learn by looking and listening, and flipped lessons let me do both.

—Vaughn, fifth grader

When I'm doing the flipped lessons, it's like I have a teacher at my house.

—Emmy, fourth grader

As you begin the drafting phase of your writing unit, you feel the pressure mounting. Your students have generated topics to write about, and many have begun to flesh out these ideas by writing notebook entries and creating outlines. Some students ask impatiently, "Can I draft it now?" But others have yet to latch on to an idea that excites them. You are experiencing again the joys and challenges of writing workshop. All writers are unique and need different lessons and amounts of time to work on concepts. It's hard to juggle everything.

You look forward to teaching minilessons about quick writing, effective leads, the structure of various genres, and elaboration. As you plan your whole-class minilessons and your one-on-one conferences, you look over your notes from the previous week. You think about your students and what each needs in the upcoming week. Kayla will need some one-on-one time with you to flesh out her outline; you hope to be able to move her quickly to the drafting phase. Maya finished her outline and began her draft during the last session; she'll need some additional support in order to keep moving forward.

You feel a little overwhelmed. Each student is working on something different. How are you going to help each writer be successful? Which whole-class minilesson will you teach? How many of your students can you talk with one-on-one during the workshop? You know if you take it one step at a time, everything will work out. But you're always looking for a better way.

Setting Goals: Why Do I Want to Flip This Lesson?

Drafting is an exciting phase of the writing process. Your students are ready to begin turning their ideas into full pieces of writing. Natalie Goldberg, author of *Writing Down the Bones* (2006), equates writing a draft with combining all the ingredients together, stirring, and creating goop. Later, during revision, we shape this goop to give it more form, but the central purpose of drafting is to put everything together and see what happens. Drafting helps students locate and use different "ingredients," or writing strategies. This work is challenging and messy, satisfying and dissatisfying to equal degrees.

Lucy Calkins (1994) recommends encouraging students to write fast and furiously when they draft, unencumbered by any sense of perfectionism. Once students have their ideas down, they can begin revising them for clarity and purpose.

Your goal is to help each student express her or his ideas. You want your students to build their stamina for writing and use their time in the workshop effectively. You envision drafting taking place in a nearly silent workshop as students pour words onto the page. Your students have many different writing styles, and flipped learning can help you address some of your instructional challenges. Flipping one or more lessons (see the decision table in Figure 3.1) will help you differentiate your instruction, create more time for those coveted one-on-one conferences, and help your students develop a sense of agency in their learning.

Think about which drafting lessons you would like to flip. Choose one or two that will be helpful to you throughout the year because students will refer to them again and again. A likely candidate is using an outline to write fast and furiously, getting it all down and not worrying about making it perfect.

> *Flipping one or more lessons will help you differentiate your instruction, create more time for those coveted one-on-one conferences, and help your students develop a sense of agency in their learning.*
>
> — Dana and Sonja

You notice students who . . .	Your goal is for them to . . .	You create a flipped lesson . . .
are struggling to begin drafting their writing	write fast and furiously in order to build their writing stamina	on writing a lot to give your students a model of flooding the paper with ideas, then have them try it themselves
have dull leads or use the same type of lead over and over	try various leads and choose their favorite	on leads that pop, describing five types of leads, each with an example students can emulate
are losing steam as they draft; the beginning is more developed than the middle or the ending	write a balanced, fully formed draft	about not fizzling out in which you share tips for maintaining writing stamina
do not use their outlines or storyboards while drafting	independently use their outlines or storyboards to keep their writing focused	titled "Outlines Are Our Superheroes" in which you model how students can use their outlines while drafting

FIGURE 3.1 ▲
Decision Table for Flipping Lessons on Drafting

Selecting Tools: How Am I Going to Flip This Lesson?

You have many choices when it comes to selecting tools. Use the Selecting Tools checklist (see Figure 2.2), keeping in mind the type of lesson you are teaching. Whether you want to film a presentation, capture a screenshot of a document, or use your cell phone to film yourself writing furiously on lined paper, there is technology that can support you. But don't put too much pressure on yourself. Do the best you can with the time you have.

The tools we selected for our model lesson on drafting are indicated on the completed Selecting Tools checklist in Figure 3.2. If you need help planning your flipped lesson, scan the QR Code in Figure 3.3 and review the components of a flipped lesson.

You can use a cell phone to capture a flipped-learning lesson if it has Internet access, a camera, and a voice recorder. For this lesson, Dana used a cell phone to film herself writing in her writing notebook. Figure 3.4 lists pros and cons related to using a cell phone for a flipped-learning lesson. For tips on how to use your cell phone to film your lesson, see Figure 3.5.

FIGURE 3.2 ▶
Selecting Tools Checklist for "Drafting: Outlines Are Our Superheros"

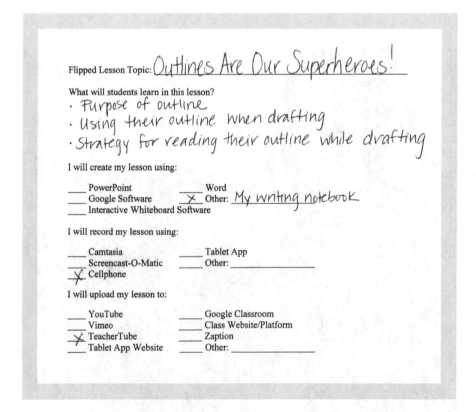

Flipped Lesson Topic: *Outlines Are Our Superheroes!*

What will students learn in this lesson?
- *Purpose of outline*
- *Using their outline when drafting*
- *Strategy for reading their outline while drafting*

I will create my lesson using:

____ PowerPoint   ____ Word
____ Google Software   _X_ Other: *My writing notebook*
____ Interactive Whiteboard Software

I will record my lesson using:

____ Camtasia   ____ Tablet App
____ Screencast-O-Matic ____ Other: _____
_X_ Cellphone

I will upload my lesson to:

____ YouTube   ____ Google Classroom
____ Vimeo   ____ Class Website/Platform
_X_ TeacherTube   ____ Zaption
____ Tablet App Website ____ Other: _____

FIGURE 3.3 ▲
QR Code for "Creating a Flipped Lesson"

FLIP YOUR WRITING WORKSHOP

Pros	Cons
> Convenient > Can film anywhere, including outdoors > Can film yourself writing in your notebook or adding to an outline or making changes > Can upload the lesson directly to sites like YouTube and TeacherTube	> No editing capabilities > Must film lesson in one take > Need some way to steady the cell phone during filming > No animation or other bells and whistles

◄ FIGURE 3.4
Pros and Cons for Using a Cell Phone to Film a Flipped-Learning Lesson

TECH**TIPS**

> Make sure you have access to the Internet.

> Use your cell phone's camera and voice recorder to film your lesson.

> Stabilize your cell phone on a platform (a stack of books, for example) so it doesn't move while filming.

> Speak clearly and practice what you are going to say beforehand.

> Be natural!

> Film your lesson in one take.

> Keep the lesson short and concise.

> When you're finished filming, upload your lesson to YouTube, TeacherTube, Vimeo, or another host site.

◄ FIGURE 3.5
Cell Phone Tips

CREATING THE LESSON | How Will I Structure This Lesson? Which Teaching Approach Will I Use?

One of the best and most authentic ways to create an exciting flipped lesson about drafting is to model writing a draft in your own writing notebook. Modeling helps motivate and engage your students. They will be intrigued by this opportunity to see your ideas unfold on the page—to see you as a fellow writer.

In this lesson, the cell phone camera captures Dana writing a paragraph based on an outline she previously created, verbalizing the decisions she makes as she does so. Students see how to use the ideas in an outline to construct the sentences that become a paragraph.

Figure 3.6 shows this model lesson as a series of still frames. Dana begins with a simple introduction stating the lesson's objectives. Next she models using her outline to help her draft with purpose. She concludes by encouraging her students to try this on their own. (Scan the QR Code in Figure 3.8 to see the filmed version.) In Figure 3.7, you can see one of her students' writing.

> " Modeling helps motivate and engage your students. They will be intrigued by this opportunity to see your ideas unfold on the page—to see you as a fellow writer. "
>
> —Dana and Sonja

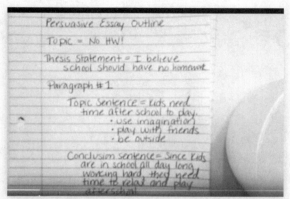

▲ **FIGURE 3.6 a** Lesson Topic

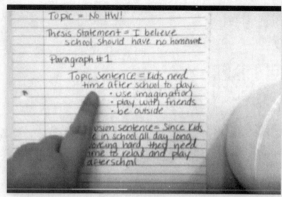

▲ **FIGURE 3.6 b** Learning Objectives

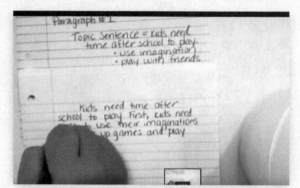

▲ **FIGURE 3.6 c** Content—Model How to Write a Draft Using an Outline

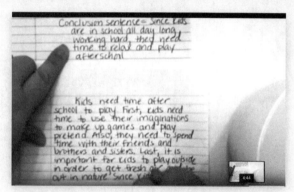

▲ **FIGURE 3.6 d** Content—Model How to Refer to an Outline While Drafting

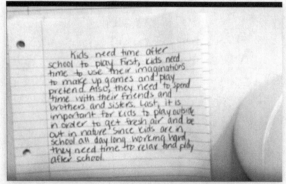

▲ **FIGURE 3.6 e** Review Process. Then, Students Try!

FIGURE 3.7 ▶
Sample Work

FIGURE 3.8 ▲
QR Code for
Sample Lesson

Caged Beasts: Bars are Never Freedom

Everyone remembers the first time they went to the circus. The leaping acrobats, the crackling popcorn, the cheering crowd, and most of all, the beautiful and enchanting elephants. People love to see elephants dressed up in sparkling garments throwing around a ball, and marching in line with one another. Though amazing in the spotlight, their treatment outside the circus tent is a growing issue. What most people don't understand is that ~~elepo~~ elephants in the circus are abused and mistreated. Elephants are taken away from their natural habitat, and crammed into train ~~cars~~ cars, faced with cruelty and a whole new life. Should circuses be keeping these wild, feral animals in the circus, or should ~~they~~ remain roaming free? Elephants should stay in the wild for three reasons.

Though many people think of the circus as pure fun, elephants can be a threat to public safety. Having such large animals confined to such a small

Determining the Method of Delivery: When and Where Will Students Use This Lesson?

Flipped learning helps students who need to

» review concepts more than once or twice before they retain them
» move forward
» be challenged
» hear explanations about how to use checklists and rubrics
» have charts explained in greater depth
» see examples and models of polished work

You might use this flipped lesson as a homework assignment for the entire class, or perhaps you have a small group of students who need additional practice with drafting or using their outlines.

Here's an example of how Dana has used the lesson.

Reviewing her conference notes, she notices that four or five students need help using their outlines when drafting. The "Outlines Are Our Superheroes" lesson is perfect for this purpose. However, instead of pulling together a small group of students, she makes the lesson available to all. Her primary goal is for her students to assess their own progress and set their own learning goals. She wants to give them opportunities to determine what they need to work on and obtain the resources they need on their own. This will help them become agents of their own learning.

At the beginning of the day's writing workshop, Dana writes, "NEW FLIPPED LESSON: Outlines Are Our Superheroes" on the whiteboard at the front of the classroom. There is a little buzz of anticipation as students notice this announcement.

She gathers her writers on the rug for a minilesson about increasing the amount of writing they will produce today. Her overall goal is to help all her students increase their writing stamina. She teaches two new strategies her students can use to increase the amount of writing they do and adds these strategies to the appropriate classroom anchor chart. Before she has her students set goals for the day, she draws their attention to the whiteboard: "Writers, we have a new flipped lesson available for you to learn from today. If you find that you are not using your outline while drafting, you will want to consider learning from this lesson. It is about how outlines are like superheroes and can help you keep your writing on track and focused."

The students go off to write. Many begin by rereading ideas in their notebooks. Some immediately start writing. A few access the flipped lesson on using outlines in the drafting phase. Dana compliments these students out loud, as a reminder to the others that the lesson is available. At the end of the session, she asks her students to jot down two things they did during the workshop; whether they accessed a flipped lesson; and what their writing goals for the next day are.

At the end of the day, Dana looks over her students' reflections and goals. The majority of the students who needed help using their outlines while drafting accessed the flipped lesson. She makes a note to touch base with them the next day about what they learned and how they might apply it in the future. She's thrilled that her students assessed their own learning needs and took steps to learn new strategies on their own, and she hopes they continue to seize these opportunities.

Creating a Formative Assessment: How Will I Know What My Students Have Learned?

There are daily opportunities to conduct formative assessments that inform our teaching and help us determine best practices. Most important, we *and* our students can use these assessments to determine what support they need. This is especially exciting in writing workshop: students can monitor their own progress by determining when they need additional resources and when they're ready for new challenges.

Flipped learning focuses on the quality rather than the quantity of what students produce in class and as homework. When asked what he liked about flipped learning, Tucker, a fifth grader, answered, "I like that you can pause the lesson so that you can go at your own speed, and I like the reflection questions in the middle of the lesson so I can answer them and know where I am."

Earlier we've described using a clipboard or some other form of note taking to collect information about students. We've described teachers recording their goals for a student and strategies the student is working on. These notes are essential in a writing workshop that uses flipped learning. We need to keep track of students' progress and the tools they use so we can understand how each child is growing not only as a writer but also as an independent learner.

Every teacher has his or her own assessment style. Year to year, the way we gather observations about our students' learning changes. One year we might use an observation grid on a clipboard; the next we might try an app on our tablet that stores our observations and thoughts. Improving the way we collect data is a good thing. It shows we care and are always looking for ways to improve our assessment practices.

Here are some formative assessment strategies you might consider:

» Jot down your observations and conference notes in a notebook.
» Use an entrance ticket (see Figure 1.4).
» Record your observations on sticky notes and store them in a folder or notebook.
» Have students create a writing plan like the one in Figure 4.10 (page 50).
» Ask students two questions at the beginning of class and use their answers to decide with whom you'll confer.
» Circle the room at the beginning of the workshop, noting what everyone is working on.

» Collect your students' writing notebooks and read what they've written.

» Work with students one-on-one to discover more about what they're working on.

One of the best ways to help your students practice formative assessment on their own work is through goal setting. We have our students set daily goals as well as goals at the end of the week. Great times for students to set daily goals during the workshop are at the end of the minilesson before they get started with their writing or at the end of the workshop period, when they can set goals for the next day. Writing goals don't have to be lengthy, and setting them needn't be cumbersome. Students can simply write their goals in the top right-hand corner of their current notebook page or on a sticky note. Students using tablets or computers can set up a document labeled "My Writing Goals" (see Figure 3.9) and enter goals there.

We also encourage our students to set goals at the end of each writing workshop, either for that night's homework or the next workshop period. Additionally, having students set goals for themselves at the end of the week helps them jump right back into their writing on Monday.

Goal setting is one way students self-advocate and reflect. All students need to know that their voices are important in the learning process, that they are equal partners in determining what it takes for them to grow as writers. Asking students to decide what they need, which steps they would like to take next, and what they would like to learn makes writing workshop a dynamic learning environment.

FIGURE 3.9 ▾
Goals Document

My Writing Goals

Date	Writing Goals

Top Five Flipped Lessons for Drafting

In addition to "Outlines Are Our Superheroes," we've had excellent results flipping the following lessons pertaining to drafting both fiction and nonfiction:

» Getting Your Thoughts Down Quickly: Building Stamina and Writing More
» Leads: Grabbing Your Reader
» Expanding Your Ideas: Strategies for Elaborating While Drafting
» Essay Introductions: What Goes in the Introduction?
» Don't Let Your Ending Fall Apart: Three Strategies for Endings That Work

We can't say enough about the benefits of having flipped lessons on hand that students can refer to again and again during the year. These lessons are lifesavers as we try to juggle all the needs of our students. We use the five listed here, as well as others, to ensure our students are able to review concepts and move forward based on their needs. Our students have reviewed "Essay Introductions" too many times to count, referring to it even when they are writing for other classes. It's worth the time it takes to create these lessons. Students use them.

Final Reflection

Flipping lessons takes trial and error. Many times we've called each other to say we're exasperated by technology and want to chuck it all. But we hang in there because we know we can figure it out. Once we've taken some time to reflect on what's worked and what is going well, we find the silver lining that encourages us to move forward. Asking questions of ourselves and our colleagues helps us develop strategies that work.

After creating one or two flipped lessons, reflect on what worked and whether you feel comfortable repeating the process. There is no need to experiment with a lot of different technological tools right away. Get good at what you know and what works for you.

Pause for a moment and think about using flipped learning during the drafting phase of writing. Jot down in your teacher journal responses to these four questions:

1. Which flipped lessons helped strengthen my students' writing stamina?
2. Are students using flipped lessons independently to improve elements of their writing and produce organized drafts?
3. What formative assessment practices am I using? Are they working?
4. How are my students setting goals? How often is this happening? Are my students using flipped lessons to accomplish their goals?

In the same way your students are drafting and getting their ideas down, you are beginning to find ways to get your flipped lessons down. As you practice, it will become faster and easier to create these lessons. You're on your way!

> *Flipped learning is a wonderful way to personalize learning for each child. As a parent, I appreciate the lessons teachers make and assign so that I can understand what my child is learning in the classroom. My daughter also has the opportunity to review material by watching the lessons as many times as she needs to. Flipped learning makes my child an active participant in her own learning. It gives her more classroom time to interact with her teacher and classmates regarding questions she may have about the flipped-learning lessons. It's a very powerful model for teaching and learning.*
>
> —Mrs. Yoshida

4

REVISING:
SEEING OUR WORK AGAIN

I like to learn from flipped lessons because I can hear my teacher's voice and see all her examples. If I'm confused I can watch them again or just the parts I need. Also, I like how the lessons stop and ask questions to make sure you get it.

—Megan, sixth grader

The school year is flying by and your students have made great gains as writers. The routines of writing workshop are set, and students are working their way through the writing process more smoothly. They're ready for a new challenge. You launch a new writing unit on feature articles. After reading extensively in this genre and noticing the structure of feature articles, students begin writing their own.

There is a steady buzz of excitement in class each day. Students have selected their topics, researched them, and decided whether to write with a partner or independently. They've spent days writing fast and furiously, capturing what they're discovering about their topics. Pages upon pages of their writing notebooks are filled with notes, and they've moved on to drafting pieces on Google Docs that they share with you so you can monitor their progress and comment on their writing.

You've created a checklist to remind students of a feature article's structural elements, which you've spent weeks noticing and discussing in class. Each day as you've moved from student to student, checking their writing, you've reminded them to use this checklist, as well as the mentor texts and the classroom anchor charts you've created together to help them write feature articles effectively.

Today, a chorus of "I'm done!" echoes through the classroom as students declare they've finished drafting. Students head off to lunch and you settle down at your desk to review their drafts. You grab a notepad and pencil to jot down what you notice about your students and their progress.

As you move from one Google Doc draft to the next, you're pleased to see that students have mastered the general shape and structure of feature articles, but you're not satisfied. You have high expectations for your students and you want them to grow and thrive as writers.

Andy and Colson have done terrific research, but their writing sounds more like an opinion essay. Bella and Amber have also gathered a great deal of information, but their ideas need to be organized and anchored by subheadings. The angle isn't clear in Sadie and Callie's feature article. Juliette needs additional support on writing a lead. And despite all the work the students have done prior to writing, Mike, Olivia, and Eddie haven't internalized the purpose and structure of feature articles at all and need to go back to square one.

The revision support your students need seems overwhelming. You are grateful it's Friday so you have the weekend to recover from what you're experiencing and prepare yourself for all the work ahead of you on Monday.

Setting Goals: Why Do I Want to Flip This Lesson?

We've all experienced the challenges of getting our students to perceive revision as a pivotal phase in the writing process. Georgia Heard, author of *The Revision Toolbox, Second Edition: Teaching Techniques That Work* (2014), urges teachers to bring the revision process to the fore in writing workshop. We can begin to do this, she suggests, by acknowledging students' feelings about revision, which can be negative. Just mentioning the word *revision* may elicit a symphony of moans and groans. Unlike the poet William Matthews, who said, "Revision isn't cleaning up after the party, revision is the party," students view this phase of the writing process as a chore—like being asked to clean their rooms or take out the trash. They understand that revision is about change, and change can be scary. A sea of anxious faces surrounds us.

The students' anxiety shifts to panic: *How do I make my work more clear? What do I remove, what stays, and what should be added? Does this mean you hate what I've written?* You try to ease their trepidation using the words of another great poet, Naomi Shihab Nye (2002): "If a teacher told me to revise, I thought that meant my writing was a broken-down car that needed to go to the repair shop. I felt insulted. I didn't realize the teacher was saying, 'Make it shine. It's worth it.'" Helping our students *re-vision* their work, to see their work again with the goal of making big-picture changes that help them convey their ideas powerfully, is daunting. For many students, getting their ideas down was a struggle and being asked to revise feels like they're being sent back to battle! Students need numerous strategies to revise proficiently. Flipped lessons help us address a wide variety of their needs and enable them to see *revision* the way Naomi Shihab Nye does: "As a beautiful word of hope."

The ways students need to revise their work are myriad. Because your students have a variety of needs and require different types of support, you can use flipped lessons to provide individualized instruction (see the decision table in Figure 4.1 for some possibilities). Flipped lessons help students practice and apply strategies that cause them to see their work in a different light and make key changes that improve their writing.

Be strategic about the topics you'd like to flip. For example, a flipped lesson on writing a lead can be helpful throughout the year as students write various kinds of essays and articles. A flipped lesson on developing an angle is more genre-specific and may be helpful during only one writing unit. Experienced flippers create a suite of lessons that can be used in many units.

A lesson we find especially helpful is "Writing Leads That Work." Students understand the importance of immediately grabbing readers' attention (an oft-repeated question is, "How do I write an interesting beginning?") and use this lesson again and again as they write research-based arguments, essays, feature articles, and reports. We use it here as the model flipped lesson on revision.

You notice students who . . .	Your goal is for them to . . .	You create a flipped lesson . . .
are having difficulty organizing their ideas	use the organization strategies you taught during minilessons	on organizing ideas that students can review and then try out in their writing
need support for writing an effective beginning, or lead	write two types of leads and decide which works best in their piece	on beginnings in which you review examples of five types of leads and the reasons the writers chose them
have not used checklists to ensure that all required elements of the genre are included in their draft	understand the structure of the genre and use the support materials provided	on purpose and structure that uses a mentor text to highlight and model the required elements of the genre
are struggling to conclude their piece	write a conclusion that best fits their piece without repeating what has already been stated	on conclusions that explains four strategies for ending a piece effectively

FIGURE 4.1 ▲
Decision Table for Flipping Lessons on Revision

Selecting Tools: How Am I Going to Flip This Lesson?

Review the software options discussed in Chapter 1 (pages 8–9). Once you've selected the lesson or lessons you plan to flip, use the Selecting Tools checklist to help you prepare. A flipped lesson doesn't have to look like a movie trailer. If a particular software or tool is convenient and you're comfortable using it, that's OK. The goal is get the lessons out there so your students can benefit from them. Although we model a variety of tools throughout this book, in the end, you get to decide what works best for you. (If you need help planning a flipped lesson, scan the QR Code in Figure 4.2 and review the components.)

"Writing Leads That Work" began with the completed Selecting Tools checklist in Figure 4.3 and uses an interactive whiteboard. Figure 4.4 lists some pros and cons regarding interactive whiteboard software. Figure 4.5 gives you some tips for filming.

FIGURE 4.3 ▶
Completed Selecting Tools Checklist

Checklist for Flipped Lesson

Lesson Topic: _Writing Leads That Work!_

What will students learn in this lesson?

- What makes a lead strong
- Options for types of leads
- Strategies for revising a lead

I will create my lesson using:
____ PowerPoint
____ Google Software
✓ Interactive Whiteboard Software

____ Word
____ Other: _____

I will record my lesson using:
____ Camtasia
____ Screencast-O-Matic
____ Cellphone

____ Tablet App
✓ Other: _Interactive Whiteboard_

I will upload my lesson to:
____ YouTube
____ Vimeo
____ TeacherTube
____ Tablet App Website

____ Google Classroom
✓ Class Website/ Platform
____ Zaption
____ Other: _____

Pros	Cons
› It's simple, easy to use, and provides clean, uncluttered visuals.	› The software needs to be downloaded to your computer; this can be pricey if you have to buy it yourself.
› You probably already know how to use it.	
› It includes effects such as highlighting and graphics.	› It's not as mobile as a cell phone, tablet, or laptop.
› You can use the interactive whiteboard pen to write while filming.	› You must film in one take.
	› You can't edit.
› You can save the lessons to your computer easily.	› The recording isn't always the best quality, especially if it includes animation.
› You can both flip the lesson and teach it live in your classroom.	

◄ FIGURE 4.4
Pros and Cons
Regarding Interactive
Whiteboard Software

TECH**TIPS**
› Create the lesson as you would any interactive whiteboard lesson.
› Test animation and other bells and whistles ahead of time; they may not film well.
› Look for a Recorder or Recording label using the menu bar.
› Film the lesson in one take. There is no editing capability.
› You can film your lesson without being hooked up to your interactive whiteboard. The software is on your computer, not the board.
› However, you can also film your lesson while at your interactive whiteboard, using the pens, highlighting tools, and so on.

◄ FIGURE 4.5
Tips for Filming a Flipped
Lesson Using Interactive
Whiteboard Software

How Will I Structure This Lesson?
Which Teaching Approach Will I Use?

We created a lesson prompting inquiry so students could examine several types of leads and investigate how and why they work. Figure 4.6 replicates the lesson's

Revising Leads

Writing Leads That Work!

▲ **FIGURE 4.6 a** Lesson Topic

Objectives:

- Learn the purpose of leads

- Strategies writers use to hook readers

- Get started!

▲ **FIGURE 4.6 b** Learning Objectives

Identifying Types of Leads

Listen to me read three different leads. In your writer's notebook, write down the approach you feel the writer has taken for each of these leads.

Example 1 - _____

Example 2 - _____

Example 3 - _____

▲ **FIGURE 4.6 c** Content—Inquiry-Based Approach

Student Example

Have you ever wondered how you would survive if you found yourself alone on a deserted island? How would you protect yourself against the elements of nature? How would you get food and water? Where would you sleep?

▲ **FIGURE 4.6 d** Content—Examine Types of Leads

Types Of Leads

Leads should be clear, interesting, and informative. There are many ways writers accomplish this.

Ways to "Lead"...

humor	question	shocking facts
scene	poem	comparison
quote	dialogue	opinion
riddle	announcement	definition

▲ **FIGURE 4.6 e** Students Try!

Trial and Success!

Experiment!

Include at least four sentences in your lead.

Try two different leads.

Share your options with a writing partner and me.

Any questions?

▲ **FIGURE 4.6 f** Assessment—Students Self-Assess Their Work and Understanding

still frames; there are only seven slides. However, inquiry requires that students examine leads in which writers use various techniques—shocking facts, a vignette, comparisons—to interest readers. Therefore, during the lesson, Sonja asks students to hit the Pause button while they explore the technique the writer is using in each type of lead. (Scan the QR Code in Figure 4.8 to see the filmed version.)

Juliette listed the types of leads she learned about during the flipped lesson. Then, she tried out two types of leads that might work better for her writing (see Figure 4.7).

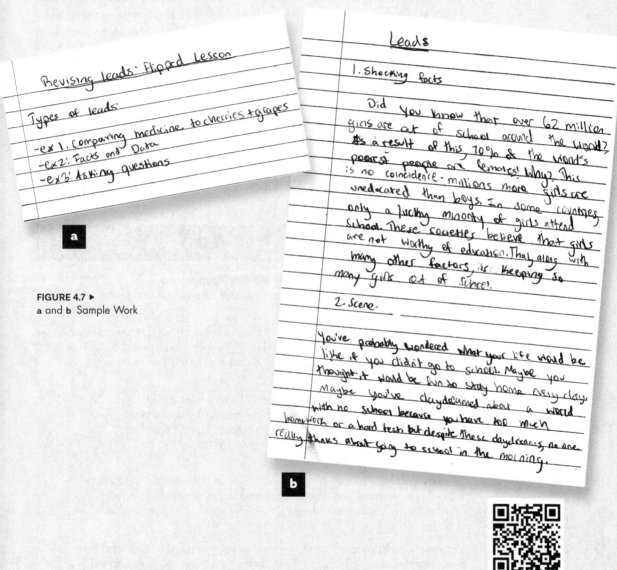

FIGURE 4.7 ▶
a and **b** Sample Work

FIGURE 4.8 ▲
QR Code for
Sample Lesson

Determining the Method of Delivery: When and Where Will Students Use This Lesson?

What we love most about flipping lessons in writing workshop is that we have tremendous range in how we use them—in class or for homework, in small groups or with individuals. They help us maximize our instruction. Figure 4.9 shows how a sample week of flipped learning might play out in the classroom.

Here's an example of how Sonja has used this flipped lesson on revising leads.

It's Monday morning after a weekend in which she has reflected on the previous week's instruction and prepared for the work ahead of her today. Her writers have a great deal of revising to do on their feature articles. Her approach today will be to have them, in groups, focus on one major revision they can make that will greatly improve their writing. As she tells her students they need to focus on just one thing, not a bunch of revisions, she notices their visible relief: they nod and smile.

As students gather their writing notebooks, Chromebooks, and other resources, Sonja groups them by the type of revision on which she'd like them to focus. Five students will work on revising their leads. She asks them to access the "Writing Leads That Work" flipped lesson and says she'll check in with them later. She asks ten students to take out their feature article checklist and use it to review their draft

FIGURE 4.9 ▼
A Sample Week of Flipped Lessons

Day	Flipped Lessons
Monday	**Small Group.** A small group works with the "Revising Leads" lesson. You check in with them after five minutes to discuss their progress and plans.
Tuesday	**Individual Work.** You announce that there are three flipped lessons available for your students to use: "Organizing Ideas," "Revising Leads," and "Conclusions." Students each make a writing plan and access the lessons they need.
Wednesday	**Individual Work and Small Group.** Students review their writing plans from the previous day and set goals. You notice that several students need to review the "Conclusions" lesson. You encourage them to do so during class time or as homework.
Thursday	**Homework.** You assign as homework a flipped lesson about using checklists and rubrics when revising. You also ask students to reread their writing after accessing the lesson and identify sections needing further revision.
Friday	**Partner Work.** Students meet with their writing partners at the start of the workshop and discuss Thursday night's homework. They set goals and begin revising their work. You encourage them to review any lesson they need to.

with a partner, taking turns highlighting each checklist item that has a corresponding section in the Google Doc draft. Whatever isn't highlighted on the checklist will become their writing plan today. She reassures them she'll check in with them soon. The final group of students need more guided instruction in reviewing the purpose and structure of feature articles and will work directly with her.

After fifteen minutes, Sonja checks in with the groups working on their own. Students who accessed the flipped lesson are each writing two different leads in their writing notebook. Peering over shoulders, she notices one student is trying a shocking-facts lead and another is writing a vignette. All five are trying out a strategy from the flipped lesson. When she asks, "How's it going?" they say that when they've finished, they will take turns sharing each of the leads they've written and giving one another feedback about which works best. She smiles and nods, expressing her satisfaction with their work and their plan.

Checking in with the rest of her students, Sonja jots down the names of students who would benefit from the flipped lesson on leads for their "just one thing" revision move tomorrow. She recalls the feeling of panic she experienced on Friday and notices how confident she feels today. Having this lesson ready to go is making it possible for her to reach more students and for those students to revise more effectively.

Creating a Formative Assessment: How Will I Know What My Students Have Learned?

Continuing to monitor and assess the effectiveness of our teaching is imperative. We find reviewing the work students do in their writing notebooks is the fastest and most informative way to assess the success of our flipped lessons. What were our students able to do as a result of this lesson? How well were they able to apply the strategy taught?

Another way to measure student growth is through a writing plan (see Figures 4.10 and 4.11). Having students identify and name the ways in which they plan to revise their work lets you know they have progressed beyond "I'm done" and understand the value of seeing their work with fresh eyes and identifying areas that need further development.

Before-and-after documentation is essential when assessing students' revision skills. The writing plan lets you compare what your students could do and the challenges they faced before the flipped lesson with what they can do after. If both you and the student can see specific areas that were reworked effectively or completely transformed, the lesson was successful.

Students must be able to name specific revision strategies and apply them from one piece of writing to the next. Many of the revision strategies students need are not limited to one genre, but can and should carry over to many different types of writing. Each time students revisit or apply strategies from a previous unit's flipped lesson is a win!

FIGURE 4.10 ▾
Blank Student Writing Plan

Student Writing Plan

Name: _____

Date: _____

MY WRITING PLAN

What do you plan to accomplish as a writer today? Be sure to turn this in as soon as it's complete.

What are your writing goals today? Be specific.	
Do you plan to access a flipped lesson? If so, which one?	
Did this lesson help you?	Yes No
If yes, how? If no, why?	
Do you need a writing conference?	Yes No

FIGURE 4.11 ▼
Completed Student
Writing Plan

Writing Plan

What do you plan to accomplish as a writer today? Be sure to turn this in as soon as it's complete.

What are your writing goals today? Be specific!	Today, I want to learn how to revise my lead, so I can make it as good as possible.
Do you plan to access a flipped lesson? If so, which one?	Revising Leads
Did this lesson help you?	(Yes) No
If yes, how? If no, why?	It helped me come up with strategies for revising my lead. It was helpful to go back to earlier in the flipped lesson so I could review the different strategies.
Do you need a writing conference?	(Yes) No I want to share my work!

> *I really like using flipped lessons in writing workshop. They let me go at my own pace, stop when I need to, and best of all, I am able to use them at home if I need to review something.*
>
> —Bella, seventh grader

Top Five Flipped Lessons for Revision

We've found that the best way to avoid the "I'm done" chorus is to anticipate that our students will often run out of steam when they are revising their work. Having several flipped lessons ready to go that students can review, whatever the genre, helps them move forward with confidence. In addition to "Writing Leads That Work," the following flipped lessons also propel our students down the road to becoming powerful revisers:

- » Be Clear and to the Point
- » Be Choosy: Choose the Right Word
- » Are You Repeating Yourself? Elaboration Versus Repetition
- » Conclusions That Work
- » Changing Tenses: Do Your Verbs Match?

Flipping these lessons lets us address the predictable revision needs of our students and teach additional lessons on revision whenever students need them.

Final Reflection

In writing workshop we encourage our students to use specific revision strategies and become confident revisers. To that end, we also need to consider the ways in which we need to revise our flipped-learning practices. The writing process is a cycle, and so is our journey as creators and implementers of flipped lessons. We need to ask: *Am I creating lessons that are effective and engaging? Is there anything I need to add?* Becoming more comfortable with the process and technology used to create flipped lessons brings new opportunities to create the most engaging, effective, and efficient writing workshops possible. Grab your teacher journal, consider your work as a reviser of flipped lessons on revision, and jot down your responses to these questions:

1. Which flipped lessons help students see the revision phase as an opportunity to strengthen their work?
2. Are my students eager to use the flipped lessons? How can I increase engagement? What's working? What's not?
3. Do I have a balance of teaching approaches in my flipped lessons: prompting inquiry, modeling strategies, thinking aloud?
4. Am I feeling limited by the technology I am using? What new tools might I want to try next?

5

EDITING:
POLISHING WITH FLARE

*It's hard to remember all of the stuff I need to fix in my writing. I like to use
flipped lessons to help me when I need to edit my work.*

— Mike, fifth grader

After your sixth conference, you finally admit there's a trend. Frustration sets in. You begin to rub your temples. Conference number seven goes similarly. Your students say they're ready to publish their final drafts, yet there are mechanical errors everywhere. Dialogue and comma rules you've taught and modeled have flown the coop. There are obvious spelling errors—so obvious that the Google Doc software has underlined them in red—but students haven't corrected them. You even spot several *I* pronouns that haven't been capitalized.

You want to celebrate all the wonderful work your students have accomplished. Their writing is filled with vivid imagery, evocative figurative language, and varied vocabulary, but the numerous mechanical errors keep you from focusing on these achievements. You close your eyes and breathe deeply to keep the tension at bay. Isn't it most important that students are able to elaborate and organize their ideas powerfully? Doesn't this take precedence? Then an epiphany: work riddled with errors distracts readers from the brilliance of the writing. Editing is not optional. It's an equal part of the writing process. Without it, ideas are muddled, communication obstructed. The lyrics of Twisted Sister's "We're Not Gonna Take It" jump into your mind, revised to first-person singular: "I'm not gonna take it! No, I ain't gonna take it! I'm not gonna take it *anymore!*"

You've tried checklists, but students have checked off as complete editing work they hadn't done. You've asked students to circle errors in colors keyed to different types of errors, the result being that their drafts have looked more like art projects than writing in progress. You've tried peer editing. You've even edited their pieces yourself, making so many changes you should have included your name in the byline! You've done everything except stand on your head to get your students to put greater emphasis on editing their writing. What's left?

Setting Goals: Why Do I Want to Flip This Lesson?

We encourage students not to become bogged down by the rules of grammar when they are generating ideas and writing a draft; the focus is on conquering the blank page and producing as much writing as possible. However, in order to present their ideas powerfully, students must be taught to revise and edit—to scrutinize their work and make cuts and corrections where needed.

Some teachers expect students to edit throughout the writing process. Others designate editing as a distinct step that happens after revising. The latter approach is particularly helpful for elementary and younger middle school students, as well as for students who struggle as writers, because it's more efficient. They have finished the major revisions and can focus on polishing their piece, rather than laboring over a sentence or paragraph that might be removed later on.

We've all used various checklists and rubrics to remind students what to look for and how to look for it. These handouts can become quite lengthy, reminding students to check spelling, capitalization, punctuation, indentation, grammar, repetition, ineffective word choice, and on and on. And students often check the boxes whether they've done the work or not. Students need to understand that editing is a matter of polishing their work and demonstrating their style as writers. They need meaningful strategies they can apply to their work.

In *Everyday Editing: Inviting Students to Develop Skill and Craft in Writer's Workshop*, Jeff Anderson (2007) reminds us that for many students, editing can be a frustrating experience that makes them feel deflated and defeated. He suggests teaching editing as a "process of invitations" that encourages students to make choices and decisions. For this approach to succeed, students need nuanced instruction they can consult again and again as they zoom in on individual sentences and words in order to improve clarity and style. Because classrooms are heterogeneous environments, students have varying needs. Some will continue to need encouragement to use periods at the end of sentences; others will be ready to use semicolons to construct more complex sentences. Carefully designed flipped lessons tailored to the specific strategies students need will help them strengthen each word, sentence, and paragraph of their writing.

They will very likely need support with spelling, punctuation, and capitalization. Isolating the type of errors made can help you target particular needs. For example, are students having difficulty with words such as *their*, *there*, and *they're*? If so, a flipped spelling lesson specifically on homophones may be needed. Or, if students are overusing and abusing commas, a flipped punctuation lesson targeting reasons to apply commas may be helpful. Use the decision table in Figure 5.1 to determine which flipped lesson (or two or three) will help your students during the editing phase.

The list of possible editing lessons is long and varied, and these lessons become increasingly complex as students reach the middle grades and beyond. Novice flippers may want to choose one lesson their students can use all year, unit to unit, genre to genre. A flipped lesson on capitalization rules is a good example. It works whether students are working toward publishing a piece or struggling to apply capitalization rules routinely. Even proficient writers require instruction on capitalization beyond the basic rules they've learned as early elementary students, so we've used it as the model lesson for this chapter. Experienced flippers may want to create a suite of flipped editing lessons.

You notice students who . . .	Your goal for them is to . . .	You create a flipped lesson . . .
have trouble remembering to apply basic punctuation rules	independently identify and correct punctuation errors in their drafts	on checking for punctuation that students can apply to each draft they write
struggle to capitalize correctly	learn capitalization rules beyond the need to capitalize the first letter of the first word of a sentence	that teaches and models which words require capital letters and which don't
need support in presenting dialogue correctly	understand how to treat dialogue and how it compares and contrasts with presenting a quotation	that provides examples of ways quotation marks are used and why
are using commas incorrectly	learn three or four comma rules they can apply to all their writing	that highlights and models several reasons for using commas

FIGURE 5.1 ▲
Decision Table for Flipping
Lessons on Editing

" *Carefully designed flipped lessons tailored to the specific strategies students need will help them strengthen each word, sentence, and paragraph of their writing.* "

— Dana and Sonja

Selecting Tools: How Am I Going to Flip This Lesson?

FIGURE 5.2 ▲
QR Code for "Creating a Flipped Lesson"

Scan the QR Code in Figure 5.2 to review software options for creating and filming a flipped lesson. The model lesson in this chapter uses PowerPoint and Camtasia (see the completed Selecting Tools checklist in Figure 5.3). Pros and cons for using PowerPoint and Camtasia are listed in Figure 5.4.

While our model lessons use various software options, remember that flipping lessons can be as easy or as elaborate as you decide. Feeling comfortable and confident will inspire you to add to your collection of flipped lessons, which will in turn benefit your students in writing workshop. We began creating lessons with Camtasia after first using Screencast-O-Matic, a cell phone, or an interactive whiteboard and feeling ready for a challenge. Camtasia gets great reviews from users, and we've found it worth the price. It's easy to film, edit, and upload the lessons, and we can make them as jazzy as we like. We won't lie: it took us many hours of playing around with the software before we felt confident using it, but it was well worth our time. After creating this lesson, we uploaded it to both YouTube and Zaption, a web application that enables users to add questions, text, and images (see the assessment section of this chapter and Figure 5.10).

Checklist for Flipped Lesson

Lesson Topic: _Capitalization_____

What will students learn in this lesson?

· When to capitalize - proper nouns vs. common nouns

· When _not_ to capitalize

· How to identify words that need editing
  for capitalization

I will create my lesson using:
✓ PowerPoint   ____ Word
____ Google Software   ____ Other: _____
____ Interactive Whiteboard Software

I will record my lesson using:
✓ Camtasia   ____ Tablet App
____ Screencast-O-Matic   ____ Other: _____
____ Cellphone

I will upload my lesson to:
✓ YouTube   ____ Google Classroom
____ Vimeo   ____ Class Website/ Platform
____ TeacherTube   ✓ Zaption
____ Tablet App Website   ____ Other: _____

FIGURE 5.3 ▲
Completed Selecting
Tools Checklist

	Pros	Cons
PowerPoint	- Very easy to use - Many options - Clean, clutter-free slides - Smooth transitions between slides - Can include animation - Easy to save to computer or tablet - Free tutorials	- Number of options can feel overwhelming - Pricey
Camtasia	- Easy to install - Free tutorials - Allows editing - Can film as many takes as necessary - Offers filming options— your screen, yourself - Can also record audio - Can add other media (songs, movie or documentary clips) - Easy to upload lessons to sites like YouTube, Vimeo, and TeacherTube - Lots of bells and whistles— callouts, arrows, animation	- Pricey - Number of options can feel overwhelming - Takes some time to learn how to use

FIGURE 5.4 ▲
Pros and Cons for Using
PowerPoint and Camtasia

My daughter can feel anxious at school because she doesn't always remember what she has learned. Her teachers have always encouraged her to use charts, but she is more of an auditory learner. Flipped lessons have helped her because she can see and hear her teacher talk her through the steps and explain the concept. She likes to use the lessons to preview and learn writing strategies, as well as review old ones.

— Mr. Lewis

CREATING THE LESSON

How Will I Structure This Lesson?
Which Teaching Approach Will I Use?

We created this lesson for second and third graders. Since our students were already applying several basic capitalization rules proficiently, this lesson differentiates instruction by introducing new strategies and allowing time for students to implement each one. Still frames of the PowerPoint slides are shown in Figure 5.5; scan the QR Code in Figure 5.6 to see the filmed version. Tips for using Camtasia are presented in Figure 5.7.

Bella applied the information she learned in this flipped lesson to her draft. She identified the proper nouns that needed capitalizing and edited her writing accordingly (see Figure 5.8).

To Capitalize or NOT to Capitalize?

▲ **FIGURE 5.5a** Lesson Topic

Objectives

- Learn the difference between proper nouns and common nouns
- Learn when a word needs to be capitalized

▲ **FIGURE 5.5b** Learning Objectives

Proper Nouns vs Common Nouns

Proper Nouns	Common Nouns
• Mrs. Cherry-Paul	• teacher
• New York	• state
• McDonald's	• restaurant

▲ **FIGURE 5.5c** Activate Prior Knowledge

New to Capitalize!

- States: New York, Connecticut, Pennsylvania
- Cities: New York City, Stamford, Philadelphia
- Countries: United States of America, Canada

▲ **FIGURE 5.5d** Introduce New Material

You try!

▲ **FIGURE 5.5e** Students Try!

You try!

▲ **FIGURE 5.5f** Students Self-Assess Their Work and Understanding

◄ **FIGURE 5.6**
QR Code for Sample Lesson

FIGURE 5.7 ▶
Tips for Using Camtasia

TECH**TIPS**
➤ The screencasting tool can film your entire screen or only a portion of it.

➤ Don't be afraid to start over; you can combine takes later.

➤ Add captions and titles using the appropriate features.

➤ Jazz things up with callouts and illustrations.

➤ Animate arrows pointing to concepts you want to emphasize.

➤ Add music.

➤ Try something new for each lesson. See what it can do!

FIGURE 5.8 ▶
Sample Work

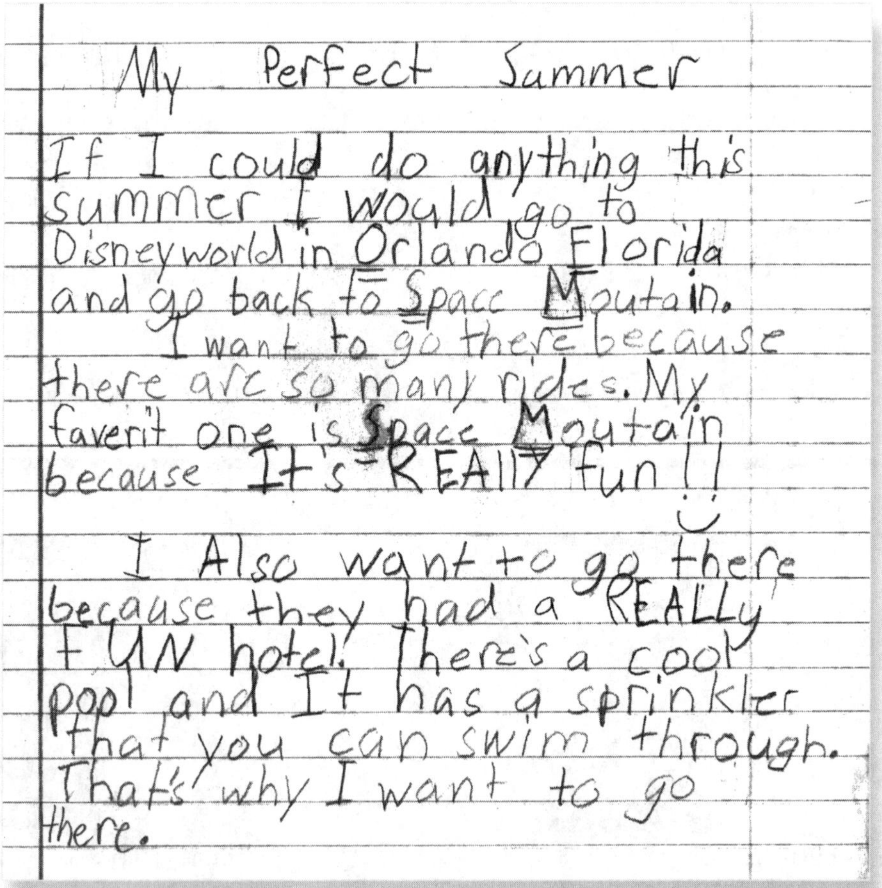

My Perfect Summer

If I could do anything this summer I would go to Disneyworld in Orlando Florida and go back to Space Moutain.
I want to go there because there are so many rides. My faverit one is Space Moutain because It's REALLY fun!!

I Also want to go there because they had a REALLY FUN hotel! There's a cool pool and It has a sprinkler that you can swim through. That's why I want to go there.

Determining the Method of Delivery: When and Where Will Students Use This Lesson?

Flipped lessons in writing workshop provide flexibility for both you and your students, as students negotiate the writing process at a variety of levels and with different needs. Flipped lessons make it much more possible to achieve your goals.

Here's an example of how Sonja has implemented this flipped lesson on capitalization.

Noticing that many students are ready to begin editing, she teaches a minilesson on the types of mechanical errors to look for. Highlighting capitalization as a particular focus, she asks that each student access the flipped lesson on capitalization as part of her or his editing process. On a classroom wall hangs a chart capsulizing the minilesson, a master checklist for what students have been asked to accomplish in their writing.

Before students begin working, Sonja has them each complete a writing plan for the day and turn it in. Glancing quickly at each plan, she sees that while several students are still revising their drafts, the remaining class members are editing their pieces. Her plan is for the majority of the class to work independently. Some students are focusing on spelling corrections. Others are using a thesaurus to combat repetitive or weak vocabulary. Three students want to confer with her about using commas. Five students have grabbed headphones to access the flipped lesson on capitalization.

After teaching two rules to the students wondering about commas, Sonja sends them off to apply this instruction to their drafts. Now she's able to check in with other students, particularly those who have been editing. Moving around the classroom, she observes students pausing the flipped lesson and scanning their drafts. Peering over shoulders, she sees drafts marked with several changes. She interrupts the class to announce, "Your drafts look good and messy! Just the way they should when you're editing. Great job, writers!" The students still have several corrections to make, but the flipped lesson slows them down and encourages them to edit more carefully. Students are inspecting their work more effectively during the editing phase and doing so independently.

Now let's examine this same sample workshop session from the perspective of Bella, a student in Sonja's classroom, as she creates her writing plan, uses the flipped lesson, and works one-on-one with Sonja:

» **10:00.** Bella gathers with her classmates on the carpet in front of Sonja, bringing her writing notebook and pencil with her, and participates in Sonja's minilesson on errors to look for.

» **10:04.** Bella creates her writing plan. Her two goals for the workshop are to

1. Review the flipped lesson on capitalization and

2. Edit her writing for spelling with her writing partner.

» **10:07.** Bella accesses the flipped lesson on capitalization.

» **10:12.** Bella rereads her writing in order to apply what she's learned in the flipped lesson.

» **10:17.** Bella meets with her writing partner; they exchange drafts and edit them for spelling.

» **10:30.** Bella meets one-on-one with Sonja. They review her writing plan for the day, and Bella points to areas in her writing where she made edits in capitalization and spelling. She's met her goals, and Sonja and Bella create a new writing plan. Bella is confident she can move on to the publishing phase of writing and asks if there are flipped lessons about publishing. There are!

» **10:36.** Bella accesses a flipped lesson titled "What Is Publishing?" and plans how she might publish her work.

» **10:50.** Bella and her writing partner share their progress and plans for tomorrow's workshop. Bella is excited and eager to keep moving forward!

Creating a Formative Assessment: How Will I Know What My Students Have Learned?

When assessing the effectiveness of your flipped editing lessons, track both the type and the number of errors in your students' work. A steadily decreasing number of errors from one assignment to the next is one indicator that your lessons are successful. Another way to measure the success of flipped editing lessons is to monitor how many times students use them during the year. Frequent use tells you that your students view editing as an essential, routine practice in writing workshop.

Most important, you want your students to monitor their progress as editors and determine for themselves the areas in which they need help and the areas in which they are accomplished. Editing rubrics that don't simply require students to check off boxes but ask them to demonstrate their understanding are most helpful. Rubrics should focus on just two or three concepts and be able to be used in many writing units during the year (see the example in Figure 5.9). This way, students aren't overwhelmed by a laundry list of items and can celebrate specific aspects of their editing work. When the focus shifts from red flags to green lights, students feel proud of their work.

You can also assess your students through an online platform such as Zaption. At www.zaption.com, you can create a free account, upload your lessons from YouTube or a similar site, and add additional features such as quizzes, reflection questions, fill-in-the-blank statements, and multiple-choice questions that make your flipped lessons interactive. Students are engaged and have additional ways to reflect on their understanding of the content. The extra step (Camtasia to YouTube to Zaption) is worth it. Tips for using Zaption (which can be accessed from computers, cell phones, and tablets) are listed in Figure 5.10. (Zaption has an online tutorial; check it out and see whether the platform is right for you.)

> *Most important, you want your students to monitor their progress as editors and determine for themselves the areas in which they need help and the areas in which they are accomplished.*
>
> —Dana and Sonja

FIGURE 5.9 ▶
Editing Rubric Focused
on Demonstrating
Understanding

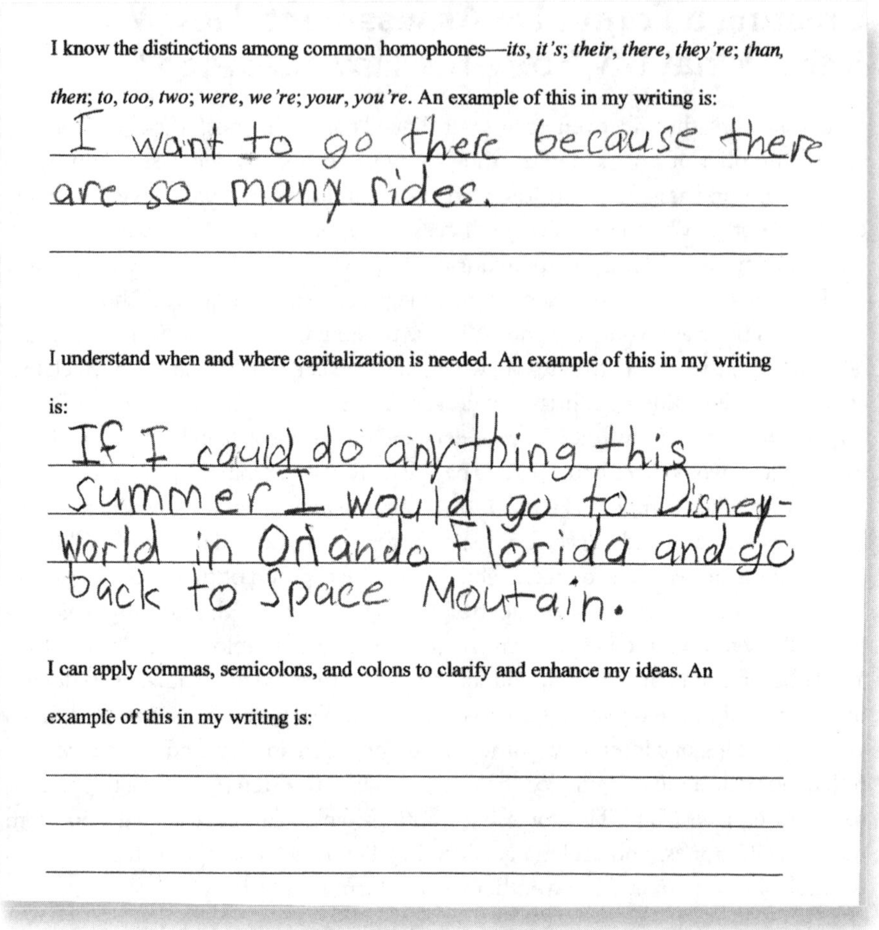

I know the distinctions among common homophones—*its, it's; their, there, they're; than,*

then; to, too, two; were, we're; your, you're. An example of this in my writing is:

> I want to go there because there
> are so many rides.

I understand when and where capitalization is needed. An example of this in my writing

is:

> If I could do anything this
> summer I would go to Disney-
> world in Orlando Florida and go
> back to Space Moutain.

I can apply commas, semicolons, and colons to clarify and enhance my ideas. An

example of this in my writing is:

FIGURE 5.10 ▶
Tips for Using Zaption

TECH**TIPS**

> Pause students at key points in the flipped lesson and have them answer multiple-choice questions, complete fill-in-the-blank statements, or take quizzes.

> Include a survey.

> Have students set goals and reflect on whether they've achieved them.

> Ask students to provide feedback.

> Add additional multimedia.

> *Sometimes I need to write in different ways, at different lengths, and at different speeds. I feel that flipped lessons help slower workers like me, as well as all the faster workers. There are many different parts of a topic that can cause confusion, like using commas. With flipped lessons, I'm able to pick and choose which lessons work best for me and my writing.*
>
> —Juliette, seventh grader

Top Five Flipped Lessons for Editing

Students need to accomplish a number of things while editing. It can be challenging for younger students and struggling writers to remember all the strategies they've been taught and how to apply them to their writing. Flipped lessons can make a big difference. In addition to being gateways to new concepts and strategies, they can be used again and again.

Tracking and analyzing the types of errors students make in their writing will help you determine which lessons will be most helpful. This in turn will help you manage your writing workshop and address student needs. We've found the following five flipped editing lessons particularly helpful:

- » Check It Out! Using Checklists Effectively to Improve Writing
- » Spelling Tips for Prefixes and Suffixes
- » Dialogue Rules: Who Said It and How?
- » Commas for Clarity
- » Critique Versus Criticism: My Role as a Peer Editor

Final Reflection

This is a great time to reflect on the progress you've made with creating flipped lessons. Perhaps you need to be more precise in how you teach a strategy. Maybe the pace of a lesson is too fast or too slow or the method you've used to implement the lesson is not working. Reflect on the following questions in your teacher journal before moving on to the next chapter:

1. What's working? What isn't?
2. What additions or deletions do I need to make to the flipped editing lessons I'm creating?
3. Are my students meeting their goals? Do they feel that flipped learning is helping them edit more effectively?
4. How are students using the flipped lessons—homework? small-group work? independently? Is this working?
5. What evidence do I have that my students are learning how to edit their writing?
6. What will I do about my students who have not applied lessons successfully?

6

PUBLISHING: REFLECTING AND CELEBRATING

What I like about flipped lessons is how descriptive they are. I use them at school and at home to see some examples and learn new things. Teachers making flipped lessons for the first time should speak clearly, make them interactive, and have loads of examples. Also, there should always be time for questions in class, because I usually have some.

—Tyler, fifth grader

As your writing workshop unit comes to a close, you feel the excitement level rising. Although the process has at times been tiring and overwhelming, you are proud of your students' progress. They generated ideas, drafted, revised, and are finishing their final edits. Looking over your notes, you notice that each student has had moments of success. You are reminded of Katherine Bomer's book *Hidden Gems*, because you have seen these gems in your students' writing. Some have made large leaps in learning, others small. You're looking forward to celebrating their success.

You look around your classroom. Some students are editing their work; some are still revising; the rest are saying, "I've finished. What do I do now?" You've heard this phrase many times throughout the unit. In earlier sessions you've encouraged these students to review related charts, expand a section of their piece, or review their work against a checklist. Now, with the writing celebration date on the calendar, you happily answer, "That's wonderful! Congratulations! It's time for you to publish your writing."

Phew! That feels good! But now your students are asking, "What do I have to do to publish this? What does that mean?" You will need to spend the majority of your time with the students who are still revising and editing. How can you help your students who are eager to publish?

You brainstorm a list of what you hope they will learn in the publishing phase of the writing process. For one thing, you expect them to take pride in how they present their work. Perhaps this will include a cover page and a list of references? Maybe you'll let them choose how they will present their work—a printed document? an e-book? a blog post? You also want them to read a portion of their work aloud, which will mean practicing their public speaking skills. Last, you expect your students to give one another positive feedback on their writing. This will necessitate lessons about how to listen carefully and notice the gems in one another's work. Faced with all these hopes for your final celebration, you begin to worry: your students are in so many different places in their writing, they may not all be ready for the celebration.

Setting Goals: Why Do I Want to Flip This Lesson?

Publishing and celebrating writing often receives little attention. We confess to taking shortcuts here, simply asking students to hand in their final copies. Time is precious. Maybe we tack these final pieces on the bulletin board, but without asking the authors to talk about them first. The pieces hang there for a couple of weeks; maybe someone stops to read them, maybe not. We grade the papers, write some comments on them, and hand them back. Students read the comments, look at the grade, maybe stick the piece in the back of their writing folder, or maybe toss it in the recycle bin. That's no way for their hard work to end!

Publishing and celebrating students' work is worth the time it takes. Just like published authors, students want to share their hard work with others. Doing so not only increases students' desire to put forth their best work but also creates a community of writers. Students see their classmates as fellow writers who can help them be successful, and cheer them on through challenges.

Your goals during the publishing phase are to help students present their ideas with pride and celebrate their work. Flipping one or more lessons will allow you to balance the needs of all your students. You can work with students who are still revising and editing while students who are ready to publish move forward at their own pace. When the revisers and editors reach the publishing stage, they too can learn from the flipped lessons.

Students need to present their work for peer feedback. Just as each student has a distinct writing style, each also wants to share his or her writing in a different way, a wish that we need to respect. Writing can be deeply personal. Some writers may choose to share very little of what they've written, while others enjoy the spotlight. Some students wave their hand in the air while yelling, "I want to go first!" Others are hesitant and reserved about sharing their work in a group. Flipped learning can address some of these differences. Use the decision table in Figure 6.1 to decide whether flipping one or more lessons will help your students in the publishing and celebrating phase of your writing workshop.

The best flipped publishing lessons provide examples and models that inspire students to publish their work in interesting ways. Students who struggle with public speaking also benefit from flipped lessons on this skill. Parents often tell us their children use these tips at home when they practice reading their writing. We love hearing this! Who wouldn't feel more comfortable practicing in the mirror at home rather than in a corner of the classroom? Flipped lessons help students work on what they need in the comfort of their home at a time convenient for them.

Our model flipped publishing and celebrating lesson is "Being an Awesome Writing Partner: Feedback Every Writer Will Appreciate."

You notice students who . . .	Your goal for them is to . . .	You create a flipped lesson . . .
have no idea where to begin; they don't know what publishing entails	know what published writing in the genre they've been working in looks like	that provides examples of published pieces
are anxious about reading their piece aloud	learn public speaking tips: practice reading the piece aloud, read with expression, make eye contact with the audience, speak loudly and clearly	that presents five tips for public speaking
need tips for giving helpful peer feedback and positive comments	give their classmates specific examples of what they enjoyed about the writing	that will help your writers take their peer feedback from good to great
haven't included all the elements of a finished piece (e.g., cover page, essay, reference list)	independently use checklists to gather all the components of the writing project	that will help students organize their work and check it for completeness

FIGURE 6.1 ▲
Decision Table for Flipping Publishing Lessons

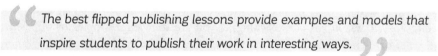

The best flipped publishing lessons provide examples and models that inspire students to publish their work in interesting ways.

—Dana and Sonja

Selecting Tools: How Am I Going to Flip This Lesson?

Use the technology that works best for you, but keep in mind which tools are best suited to the lesson you are teaching. If you are showing examples of published pieces written by former students, you can use a cell phone or tablet camera to film them. However, if you are creating a lesson on public speaking tips, you may want to make a PowerPoint presentation. As always, you want to create lessons that are personable and inviting. You want to engage your learners! (Refer to Chapter 1 if you need to review the options for helpful hardware and software.)

We created the model lesson using a free tablet app called Explain Everything (see the completed Selecting Tools Checklist in Figure 6.2). We put together a simple presentation using the app's features, then hit Record. (Always keep a flipped lesson short; don't turn it into a lengthy lecture. This is a writing workshop minilesson—*mini* being key.) We then uploaded it to YouTube and from there to Zaption. (The app also comes with its own online upload site; you can store flipped lessons there for a fee.) For tips about creating a flipped lesson, scan the QR Code in Figure 6.3; for the pros and cons of using an app, see Figure 6.4.

Flipped Lesson Topic: _Feedback from Writing Partners_

What will students learn in this lesson?

· _3 ways to give meaningful, positive feedback_

·

·

I will create my lesson using:

_____ PowerPoint _____ Word
_____ Google Software __X__ Other: _Explain Everything app_
_____ Interactive Whiteboard Software

I will record my lesson using:

_____ Camtasia __X__ Tablet App — _Explain Everything_
_____ Screencast-O-Matic _____ Other: _____
_____ Cellphone

I will upload my lesson to:

__X__ YouTube _____ Google Classroom
_____ Vimeo _____ Class Website/Platform
_____ TeacherTube _____ Zaption
_____ Tablet App Website _____ Other: _____

FIGURE 6.2 ▲
Completed Selecting Tools Checklist

FIGURE 6.3 ▲
QR Code for "Creating
a Flipped Lesson"

◄ **FIGURE 6.4**
Pros and Cons of
Using an App

Pros	Cons
❯ Convenient and easy	❯ Must film in one take
❯ Students can use it to create flipped lessons too	❯ Limited editing
❯ Includes fun tools	❯ Some apps cost money
❯ Free online tutorial on how to use the app's features	❯ Some apps allow you to store your lessons on their online sites, but check the pricing and storage restrictions
❯ Easy to upload to YouTube, etc.	

CREATING THE LESSON | How Will I Structure This Lesson? Which Teaching Approach Will I Use?

This lesson models how to read a piece of writing aloud and provide positive feedback. It also provides a few sentence starters to use when giving feedback. The modeling approach allows us to enumerate the steps, provide an example, and highlight tools students can use when they do this work on their own. The lesson contains only a few slides (see the still frames in Figure 6.5), which keeps the pace quick and focused. Scan the QR Code in Figure 6.6 to see the filmed version. Examples of the feedback students gave one another (on sticky notes) are included in Figure 6.7.

▲ **FIGURE 6.5a** Lesson Topic

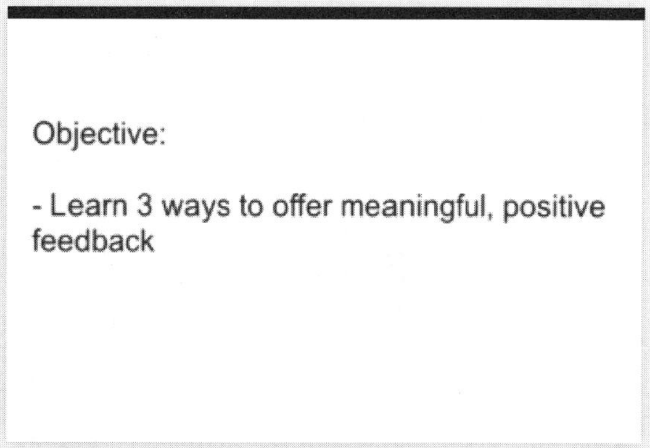

Objective:

- Learn 3 ways to offer meaningful, positive feedback

▲ **FIGURE 6.5b** Learning Objectives

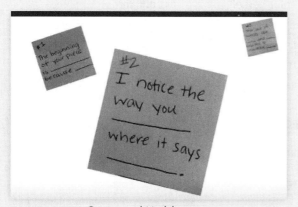

▲ **FIGURE 6.5c** Content and Modeling

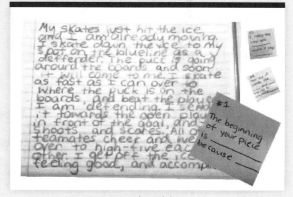

▲ **FIGURE 6.5d** Content and Modeling

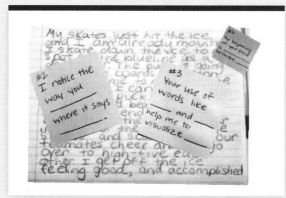

▲ **FIGURE 6.5e** Students Try!

FIGURE 6.6 ▲
QR Code for
Sample Lesson

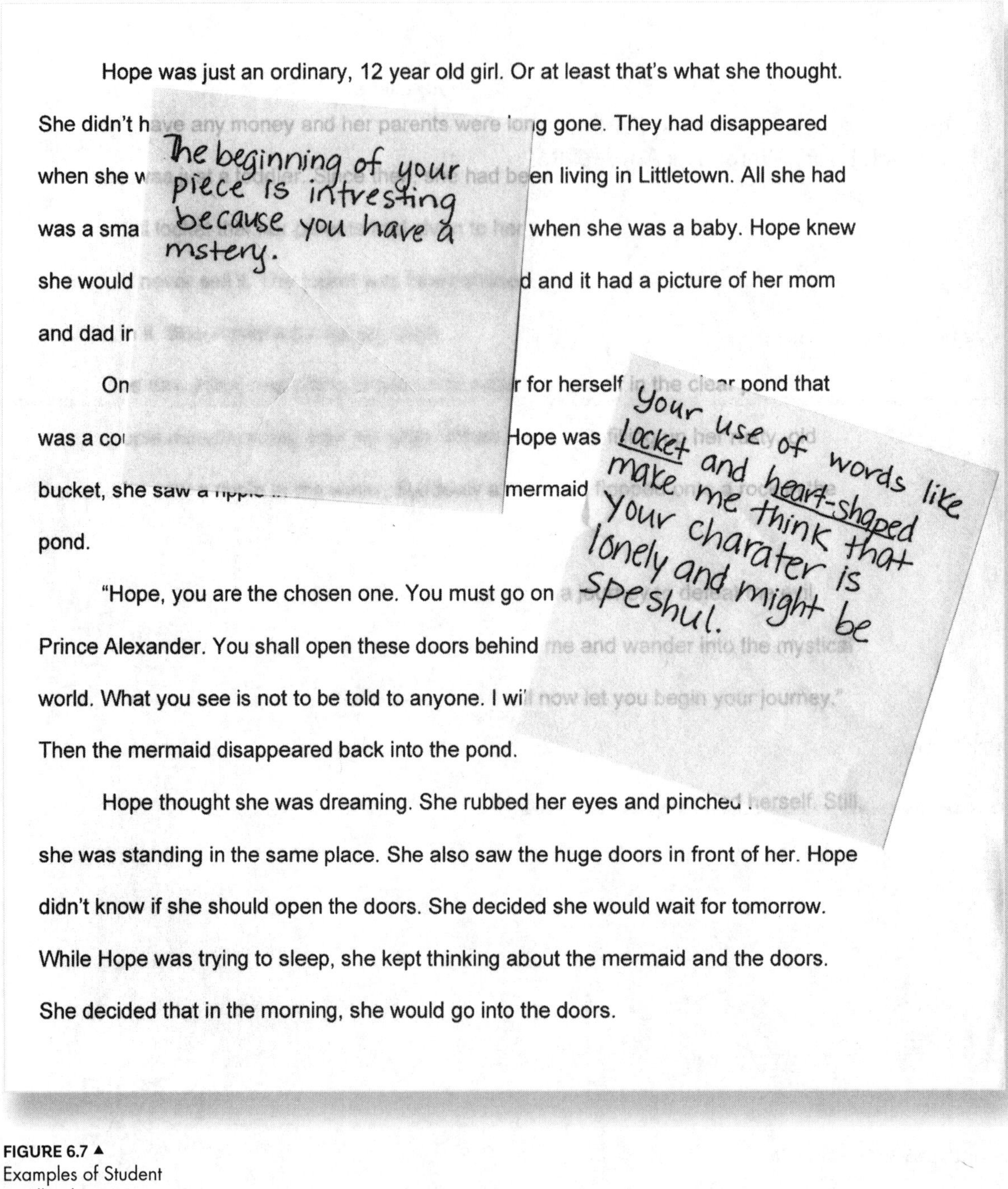

Hope was just an ordinary, 12 year old girl. Or at least that's what she thought.

She didn't h~~ave any money and her parents were~~ lo~~n~~g gone. They had disappeared

when she w~~as~~ *The beginning of your piece is intresting because you have a mstery.* ~~had be~~en living in Littletown. All she had

was a sma~~ll~~ when she was a baby. Hope knew

she would ~~d and it had a picture of her mom

and dad ir

On~~ ~~r for herself ~~in the clear~~ pond that

was a co~~ Hope was *Your use of words like locket and heart-shaped make me think that your charater is lonely and might be speshul.*

bucket, she saw a ripple mermaid

pond.

"Hope, you are the chosen one. You must go on ~~ Prince Alexander. You shall open these doors behind ~~me and wander into the mystical

world. What you see is not to be told to anyone. I wi~~ll now let you begin your journey."

Then the mermaid disappeared back into the pond.

Hope thought she was dreaming. She rubbed her eyes and pinched ~~herself. Still,

she was standing in the same place. She also saw the huge doors in front of her. Hope

didn't know if she should open the doors. She decided she would wait for tomorrow.

While Hope was trying to sleep, she kept thinking about the mermaid and the doors.

She decided that in the morning, she would go into the doors.

FIGURE 6.7 ▲
Examples of Student
Feedback

Determining the Method of Delivery: When and Where Will Students Use This Lesson?

There are many options for using this flipped lesson in the classroom. You might assign it as whole-class homework; if students view this lesson the night before a writing celebration, they'll return the following day ready to give positive peer feedback. (Tips for establishing flipped-learning homework routines are provided in Figure 6.8.) Alternatively, a small group of students may need to practice giving peer feedback.

The following vignette from Dana's writing workshop demonstrates how she uses this flipped lesson during the publishing phase of the writing process.

Dana's students have generated ideas, created drafts, and revised and edited their work. They will celebrate tomorrow by sharing their work in small groups of four. Each listener will write positive comments on sticky notes. This approach encourages all the students to listen carefully to the writing and write motivational comments for the writer. It's a celebration, after all!

Dana wants to make sure all her students are prepared to give their peers positive feedback on their writing, so she calls them together in front of the interactive whiteboard. She begins by complimenting them on the final day of preparations. She's noticed their hard work. Then she introduces the homework assignment for the night. She brings the flipped lesson up on the interactive whiteboard's screen and gives her students a brief introduction: "Tonight's homework assignment includes

TECH**TIPS**
> Make sure the lesson is available to all students (on Google Drive, YouTube, a flash drive, etc.).

> Make your expectations clear. Which supplies will students need? How will they record their thinking and take notes?

> Provide alternatives (before school, during study hall, in the library, after school) for students who cannot access the lessons at home.

> Continually highlight the importance of engaging fully with the lessons and completing the assignments. This helps students become independent learners and work at their own pace.

> Always provide an opportunity for students to ask questions the following day. This is the number one request students made when using flipped lessons as homework. They need to know they will be able to ask questions or meet with you.

◄ FIGURE 6.8
Tips for Establishing Flipped-Learning Homework Routines

a flipped lesson. This lesson will help prepare you for tomorrow's celebration. You will learn how to provide positive feedback to your classmates as you listen to them read their writing. Make sure you bring your writing notebook home with you tonight, as this lesson will require you to take some notes. As always, this lesson may be found on our class blog."

Dana knows that one or two students may not do their homework—no access to technology, no time, too disorganized—so she adds, "If for some reason you do not do tonight's assignment, come to school early tomorrow morning and complete it in the library or our classroom. There are no excuses for not being prepared for our celebration."

The following morning, Dana notices that two students arrive early and access the lesson. She compliments them on their initiative and motivation, but also finds out why they weren't able to access the lesson at home. She records the reasons in her observation notes, keeping track of who has difficulty accessing the lessons versus who is disorganized and not managing time well. This way, she'll know the best way to help if this becomes a pattern.

At the beginning of the celebration, Dana says, "I am so proud of everyone's hard work during this writing unit. We have generated ideas and drafted, revised, and edited our writing. We put the final touches on our pieces and published them. Bravo!" There are cheers and hand clapping. "In celebration of our accomplishments, I would like each writer to read a portion of his or her work aloud. As each person reads, I would like all listeners to give positive feedback, as we learned from the flipped lesson. Does everyone have their sticky-note pads? If you need reminders about what types of feedback you might give, refer to your notes in your writing notebook. Let's get started!"

As Dana's students, in small groups of four, read their writing aloud, they are visibly excited and proud. Smiles, laughter, and the sound of pencils writing furiously on sticky notes fill the room. Dana is happy too. She didn't simply collect her students' writing and hang it on a board. Her writers are reading their work, talking about their writing with an audience, and reading thoughtful comments that will motivate them to continue writing. On the whole, Dana feels she's succeeded. Her students learned that the publishing phase of writing matters, and they are seeing the results of their hard work pay off as they celebrate with others.

> *I use flipped lessons everywhere—at home, at school, in the car. Even though my English teacher makes the lessons, I use them in other classes too, like history and science, because writing a paragraph or an essay there is basically the same. I'll probably keep using the lessons next year if my new teacher doesn't have any. They've got good examples and show me the steps in case I forget.*
>
> —Sarah, sixth grader

Creating a Formative Assessment: How Will I Know What My Students Have Learned?

Previous chapters have discussed the many forms assessment can take: observation, teacher-student goal setting, reading students' notebooks, interactive feedback and reflection using software such as Zaption, and of course reviewing students' writing.

Writing Conferences

Writing conferences are another powerful assessment tool. During conferences, you learn about students' progress and the steps they are taking to further their understanding of writing concepts and skills. During these one-on-one sessions, you ask students what is going well and what is not. The publishing phase of a unit is the perfect time to ask students questions about their overall experience. Even though time is precious, meet with each student prior to the celebration. Talking about his or her experience in the unit will provide valuable information that will help you assess your own teaching goals and the role of flipped learning in the classroom. You might ask questions such as these:

> » What went well for you in this unit?
> » Where did you hit a speed bump, need to slow down and learn a new strategy?
> » What surprised you during this unit?
> » How did you use the flipped lessons in this unit? What worked for you? What did not?
> » When tackling this genre of writing again, what would you do differently?

Embrace these moments. Powerful ideas can come out of these discussions, and you'll get a better sense of how your writers feel about the process. The focus is on how the writer grows, not the final grade.

Let's listen in as Dana sits down with Jessica two days before the final celebration to discuss Jessica's writing progress and goals for the future.

Dana begins. "How's everything going? Are you feeling ready for our writing celebration?"

Jessica nods. "Uh-huh. I'm done."

"That's great! I can't wait to hear you read your published piece to your writing group. Since this is the end of our unit, let's look over your writing goals and talk about the work you've been doing."

Jessica smiles and turns to her goals page. Together they read over Jessica's goals. Dana asks, "With which goals do you feel you've made the most progress?"

Pointing, Jessica says, "This one about elaborating. It was hard at the beginning to come up with more to say."

Nodding, Dana says, "So what helped you elaborate more? I remember at the beginning of the writing unit you were talking a lot with your writing partner about what else you might say. Did that help?"

"Well, Sarah helped me think of more details, but I also used the flipped lessons about elaborating. I think what helped the most was picturing it in my mind, like making it into a movie."

Dana smiles. "And did you practice the make-a-mental-movie strategy with the flipped lesson?"

"Yes, and then with Sarah."

"Reviewing strategies using the flipped lessons and then discussing them with your writing partner sounds like a good plan. As you move forward in the next writing unit, that will be a good way to help you meet your goals."

Goal Review

Students should also review their writing goals throughout the unit, evaluate whether they've met them, and write some goals for the future. The best times for students to set goals during writing workshop are at the end of the minilesson (right before they begin writing) and at the end of the workshop session (so they can write goals for the next day).

At the end of the celebration, students can write their goals for the next writing unit. You may need to provide prompts such as the following:

- » Write faster during drafting.
- » Elaborate more.
- » Don't wait until the last minute to edit.
- » Use revision checklists.
- » Take more advantage of the flipped lessons.
- » Talk to my writing partner more often.
- » Speak loudly when I read my work aloud.
- » Stay more organized throughout the unit.

Students can write these goals on the top right-hand corner of their current notebook page or on a sticky note. Students using tablets or computers can keep a running list of their goals in a document file labeled "My Writing Goals."

Setting goals, noting the completion of former goals, and discussing what is going well and what needs improvement are important steps in the learning process. The primary purpose of flipped learning is to create a dynamic learning environment in which students can meet their goals and set new ones.

Student-Created Flipped Lessons

What better way for students to reflect on what they learned than by creating flipped lessons themselves? Have your students each brainstorm a list of writing strategies they learned throughout the unit and plan a flipped lesson following the format in Figure 6.9. Review the plans, then have students create their flipped lessons and share them with their classmates.

Cell phones, iPad cameras, and iPad apps are all easy ways for students to create flipped lessons. If your students have laptops, we recommend using Screencastify on Google Chrome, a great Google app that allows students to save their flipped lessons directly to Google Drive, where you can create a shared folder of flipped lessons that all your students can download.

> *The primary purpose of flipped learning is to create a dynamic learning environment in which students can meet their goals and set new ones.*
>
> —Dana and Sonja

Student Flipped Lesson Plan

Slide 1: Introduce the title of your lesson.

Lesson Title: _____

Slide 2: State the lesson objectives.

Lesson Objectives:

1. _____

2. _____

3. _____

Slides 3–5: Teach. Draw or write what each slide below will look like.

3	4	5

Slide 6: Classmates try!

What will you ask your classmates to do?

_____

_____

_____

FLIP YOUR WRITING WORKSHOP

Top Five Flipped Lessons for Publishing and Celebrating

In addition to the model lesson on positive feedback, we've had great success flipping these five lessons:

» Publishing: What Is It? What Does It Look Like?
» Creating an E-book
» Do I Have All the Parts? Getting Organized for Publishing
» Reading Your Writing Aloud: Five Tips for Public Speaking
» Listening to Other Students' Writing: What Is Active Listening?

One of the greatest benefits of creating flipped lessons is having them on hand throughout the school year so students can refer to them over and over. Think how much time you'll save having "Reading Your Writing Aloud: Five Tips for Public Speaking" available all year. Your students will have many opportunities to interact with this lesson—and not just in writing workshop.

Final Reflection

Now that you've come to the end of this writing workshop unit, it's time to reflect on what went well and what lessons you'd like to flip in the next unit. (Perhaps you already have some in mind.) So set some goals for the future. Take a moment and reflect on the following questions:

1. How did flipped learning help all my students share and celebrate their writing in the publishing phase?
2. Which flipped lessons can I use in other units? Which lessons will be used over and over?
3. How did flipped learning help me manage my time during the publishing phase?
4. Which lessons worked better as whole-class minilessons? Which lessons worked better as flipped lessons?
5. What flipped lessons could students create themselves?

Reflection is very empowering, especially if you discuss your observations and experiences with a colleague or a friend. Fruitful conversations include sharing what worked, which technology feels comfortable, which lessons were especially useful, and how you want to use flipped learning in future units.

Frequently Asked Questions

Is flipped learning just for middle school and high school students?

No. Flipped learning can be used with students of all ages. Also, flipped learning is often limited to math and science, but it can be used in all content areas.

Does flipped learning consist only of assigning videos for homework?

No! Flipped learning reduces whole-class instructional time and empowers students to learn at their own pace and at a time best for them. Most of our students access flipped lessons during writing workshop sessions—as small-group work, partner work, or independent work. Occasionally, we assign a flipped lesson as homework. We also encourage students to review lessons at their leisure. It is important for students to know they can access these lessons at home if they need them. (See Chapter 1 for more information on how you can use flipped learning to differentiate and create an individualized learning experience for your students.)

There are so many flipped lessons already available online. Do I really have to create my own?

Yes, there are many good flipped lessons online. However, students prefer learning from lessons that their own teacher has created. View some representative flipped lessons online, then make your own. Your students will respond to your voice, your laugh, and your familiar style of teaching. They want to feel you there with them. A plus is that you can customize your lessons with references to events occurring during the school year. For example, when teaching a lesson about description, you might say, "Remember when we were outside at recess and saw the eagle perched on a tree branch, and we all stopped and stared at him for a while? We couldn't tear ourselves away. We were taking in every little detail as if we were imprinting his image on our minds." These references engage your students and personalize the learning experience.

What do I do if my school has no or very little technology?

Never fear! Great flipped learning can be delivered via mobile devices and flash drives. Simply upload your lesson to a site such as TeacherTube, YouTube, or WatchKnowLearn, and your students can access it on their mobile devices. If your students don't have mobile devices (common in the elementary grades), encourage them to take turns using any available computers at your school (perhaps one in your classroom and a few shared ones in the library). Flipped learning is very flexible. That's the beauty of it. You have many choices for how you can make it work for you.

I'm interested in flipped learning, but I'm technologically challenged and need the simplest way possible to create flipped lessons. Which is the easiest technology to use?

We wish there were an easy answer. Everyone has a different comfort zone with regard to technology, so the easiest way to flip for one teacher isn't always the easiest way for another. Overall, the easiest technology to use is probably your cell phone or tablet. You can film the lesson quickly with the mobile device and then upload the lesson to a server like YouTube or TeacherTube. These simple lessons are no-frills and are filmed in one take. If your school does not allow sites like YouTube, try uploading to Vimeo, TeacherTube, WatchKnowLearn, or Google Drive. (Chapter 3's model lesson was filmed with a mobile device.)

I feel comfortable using technology and want to make really fabulous flipped lessons. I'm ready to take risks. Which technology is for me?

If you want your flipped lessons to be jazzy and include lots of bells and whistles, Camtasia is for you. It's well worth the cost, with the capability for call-outs, overlays, and animations (check out the model lesson in Chapter 5). If you have a tight budget, try searching for Camtasia alternatives in online search engines. There are many options.

My teaching goal this year is to collaborate more with my colleagues. Can flipped learning help me do this?

Yes. Flipped learning is a great way to collaborate, bond, and get to know your colleagues better. It happened with us. We love making flipped lessons side by side. We share teaching strategies, discuss what is going well, and ask each other questions when we get stuck. Many teachers share their flipped lessons. For example, a fourth-grade teacher and a fifth-grade teacher might collaborate on creating a collection of writing lessons and each use them. Research reveals that students respond best to lessons featuring teachers with whom they are familiar, so creating and sharing lessons with teachers of other grade levels or content areas in your school is appealing. With your colleagues, brainstorm a list of lessons you know students will use over and over again, in many content areas. Flipped lessons on essay structure, how to write a single paragraph, or when to use a semicolon, for example, can be used in any subject. Whether students need to write a paragraph in history, English, math, or science, they can access the flipped lesson.

Can students create flipped lessons that they share with the class?

Yes! It's exciting for students to create a collection of flipped lessons. The only potential difficulty is their access to screencasting software or apps that record.

If your students have tablets or smartphones, it will be easy for them to create lessons. If they use computers, it may be more of a challenge to acquire screencasting software, but it's definitely doable. Screencastify is a great screencasting Google app; if your students use Google Docs or Google Slides, this is a great option. Overall, cell phones may be the easiest way. (Chapter 6 includes suggestions for making student-created lessons.)

My teaching goal this year is to incorporate more small-group learning in my writing workshop. How can flipped learning help me meet this goal?

Flipped learning is an excellent way to create more opportunities for small-group learning. Before we began flipping lessons, pulling together writing lessons for small groups of learners was a struggle. We were constantly reteaching strategies or teaching the same advanced strategies, group after group after group. Flipped learning saved us. We created a few flipped lessons we knew small groups would need over and over again (each chapter in this book includes a top-five list). Having these go-to lessons always available made things much more manageable. After the whole-class minilesson, we would pull together a small group of learners and encourage them to access a flipped lesson (Chapter 4 includes an example of how this looks in the classroom).

How do you explain flipped learning to parents?

We've found most parents are very receptive to flipped learning, because it provides opportunities to individualize their children's learning experience. We say, "Each child is a unique writer and learner, and we want to support every child's learning style. Flipped learning allows your child to access lessons online that will support his or her learning in writing workshop—review concepts as many times as needed, move forward at her or his own pace, and try new strategies. Flipped learning is just another way for your son or daughter to access instruction whenever he or she needs it. If your child is absent, needs more time to grasp a concept, or is ready for a new challenge, flipped lessons can provide this extra support."

How do you explain flipped learning to administrators?

Administrators welcome flipped learning, because it's a way to maximize instructional time and break away from a lockstep teaching approach. We explain flipped learning to our administrators this way: "Flipped learning is a teaching method that can be used in school or at home. Through it, students access a variety of lessons in which they review concepts, work at their own pace, and move ahead. Flipped learning helps us address our students' needs by fostering differentiated instruction, increasing time for one-on-one teaching, and strengthening student engagement." Use your administrators' receptivity to your advantage by asking for their support in securing additional technology to make flipped learning even more accessible in your classroom.

Appendix

Organizer for Planning a Flipped Writing Workshop Lesson

Lesson Topic: _____

1. Set goals. (Why do I want to flip this lesson?)

-

-

-

-

2. Select tools. (How am I going to flip this lesson?)

[Refer to Figure 2.2: Selecting Tools Checklist for more ideas.]

____ PowerPoint   ____ Word

____ Google software   ____ Other: _____

____ Interactive whiteboard software

I will record my lesson using: _____

I will upload my lesson to: _____

May be photocopied for classroom use. © 2016 by Dana Johansen and Sonja Cherry-Paul from *Flip Your Writing Workshop*. Portsmouth, NH: Heinemann.

3. Create the lesson outline. (How will I structure this lesson? Which teaching approach will I use?)

Lesson Title (Slide 1)	
Students Will Learn . . . (Slide 2)	
Teaching Points (Slides 3–5)	
Students Try!	
Reflection: How Did It Go? (Final Slide)	

4. Determine the method of delivery. (When and where will students use this flipped lesson?)

____ Individual work   ____ Homework

____ Partner work   ____ Other: _____

____ Small-group work

5. Create a formative assessment. (How will I know what my students have learned?)

____ Entrance ticket   ____ Writing notebook

____ Graphic organizer   ____ Other: _____

____ One-on-one conference

References

Anderson, Jeff. 2007. *Everyday Editing: Inviting Students to Develop Skill and Craft in Writer's Workshop*. Portland, ME: Stenhouse.

Archer, Anita L., and Charles A. Hughes. 2011. *Explicit Instruction: Effective and Efficient Teaching*. New York: Guilford.

Arnaud, Celia H. 2013. "Flipping Chemistry Classrooms." *Chemical and Engineering News* 91 (12): 41.

Atwell, Nancie. 1987. *In the Middle: Writing, Reading, and Learning with Adolescents*. Portsmouth, NH: Heinemann.

Bergmann, Jon, Jerry Overmyer, and Brett Wilie. 2011. "The Flipped Class: What It Is and What It Is Not." *The Daily Riff*. Retrieved April 14, 2014 from www.thedailyriff.com/articles/the-flipped-class-conversation-689.php.

Bergmann, Jon, and Aaron Sams. 2012. *Flip Your Classroom: Reach Every Student in Every Class Every Day*. Eugene, OR: International Society for Technology in Education.

———. 2014. *Flipped Learning: Gateway to Student Engagement*. Eugene, OR: International Society for Technology in Education.

Bomer, Katherine. *Hidden Gems: Naming and Teaching from the Brilliance in Every Student's Writing*. 2010. Portsmouth, NH: Heinemann.

Calkins, Lucy. 1994. *The Art of Teaching Writing*. Portsmouth, NH: Heinemann.

Cockrum, Troy. 2014. *Flipping Your English Class to Reach All Learners: Strategies and Lesson Plans*. New York: Routledge.

Flipped Learning Network. 2014. "Flipped Learning Network Unveils Formal Definition of Flipped Learning." Press release. Retrieved April 28, 2014, from www.flippedlearning.org/domain/46.

Fountas, Irene C., and Gay Su Pinnell. 2001. *Guiding Readers and Writers in Grades 3–6*. Portsmouth, NH: Heinemann.

Goldberg, Natalie. 2006. *Writing Down the Bones: Freeing the Writer Within*. Boston: Shambhala.

Graves, Donald. 2003. *Writing: Teachers and Children at Work*. Portsmouth, NH: Heinemann.

Heard, Georgia. 2014. *The Revision Toolbox, Second Edition: Teaching Techniques That Work*. Portsmouth, NH: Heinemann.

Hicks, Troy. 2009. *The Digital Writing Workshop*. Portsmouth, NH: Heinemann.

Leicht, Robert, Sarah Zappe, John Messner, and Thomas Litzinger. 2012. "Employing the Classroom Flip to Move 'Lecture' Out of the Classroom." *Journal of Applications and Practices in Engineering Education* 3 (1): 19–31.

Nye, Naomi Shihab. 2002. "To My Dear Writing Friends." In *Seeing the Blue Between: Advice and Inspiration for Young Poets*, compiled by Paul Janeczko, 86-87. Cambridge: Candlewick Press.

Rosenshine, Barak V. 1987. "Explicit Teaching and Teacher Training." *Journal of Teacher Education* 38 (3): 34–36.

Talley, Cheryl, and Stephen Scherer. 2013. "The Enhanced Flipped Classroom: Increasing Academic Performance with Student-Recorded Lectures and Practice Testing in a 'Flipped' STEM Course." *Journal of Negro Education* 82 (3): 339–47.

Tomlinson, Carol, and Marcia Imbeau. 2010. *Leading and Managing a Differentiated Classroom*. Alexandria, VA: Association for Supervision and Curriculum Development.

Tucker, Catlin R. 2012. *Blended Learning in Grades 4–12: Leveraging the Power of Technology to Create Student-Centered Classrooms*. Thousand Oaks, CA: Corwin.